646.47 G466m

Y0-CUQ-308

j646.47
G466
m

7778542

4/78

ARLINGTON

Memphis and Shelby
County Public Library and
Information Center

For the Residents
of
Memphis and Shelby County

ALICE GILBREATH

MAKING COSTUMES FOR PARTIES, PLAYS, AND HOLIDAYS

pictures by Timothy Evans

William Morrow and Company
New York 1974

Copyright © 1974 by Alice Gilbreath
All rights reserved. No part of this book may be reproduced or utilized in any form or by any means, electronic or mechanical, including photocopying, recording or by any information storage and retrieval system, without permission in writing from the Publisher. Inquiries should be addressed to William Morrow and Company, Inc., 105 Madison Ave., New York, N. Y. 10016. Printed in the United States of America.
    4   5   78   77   76

Library of Congress Cataloging in Publication Data

Gilbreath, Alice Thompson.
    Making costumes for parties, plays, and holidays.

    SUMMARY: Instructions for making a variety of costumes from easily available materials.

    1. Costume—Juvenile literature. [1. Costume] I. Evans, Timothy, illus. II. Title.
TT633.G53   646.4′7   73-13996
ISBN 0-688-20103-2
ISBN 0-688-30103-7 (lib. bdg.)

BY THE SAME AUTHOR:
Spouts, Lids, and Cans

CONTENTS

Introduction   5

Ghost   9

Scarecrow   11

Longhorn Steer   13

Devil   17

Spaceman   19

Octopus   23

Tree   27

Record Player   31

Robot   35

Gingerbread Boy   39

Grandfather Clock   43

Angel   47

Valentine   53

Butterfly   57

Frog   61

Bunny   65

Firecracker   71

Redheaded Woodpecker   75

Poodle   79

Indian   85

Dragon   91

To my daughter,
Tommie Sue,
with much love and gratitude
for her help and encouragement.

INTRODUCTION

Children, teachers, and youth leaders will find here a variety of costumes that can be made for parties, plays, and holidays. Most of the materials are readily available and inexpensive. Many are produced from scrap materials and boxes.

Some of the costumes are very simple to put together, and some, for older readers, will present more of a challenge. They appear in order of difficulty, progressing from those that beginners can handle easily to those that need more time and detailed work. All of the costumes that require sewing can be done by hand. However, you can use a sewing machine, if you know how, on many of them.

If the costume is to be worn only once, make it quickly and do not bother with hems, finishing details, and permanent fasteners. If it is to be worn many times, work on it more carefully. Costumes that do not have a mouth opening are not suggested for parties where refreshments will be served.

If you do not have the specific material, equipment, and tools listed, find something else to use instead. Don't be afraid to substitute.

SEWING:

Cut all patterns and material on a flat surface such as the floor or dining-room table. Never cut on a bed or a rug. The running stitch, a small even stitch about $1/4$ inch long, run in and out, is used for most hand sewing. The basting stitch, a loose even stitch about ½ inch long, is used to join costume sections together before the permanent sewing, and for gathering. In the overcast stitch (used for the butterfly costume), the thread is drawn up through the material and cast over the wire in long loose stitches about ½ inch apart.

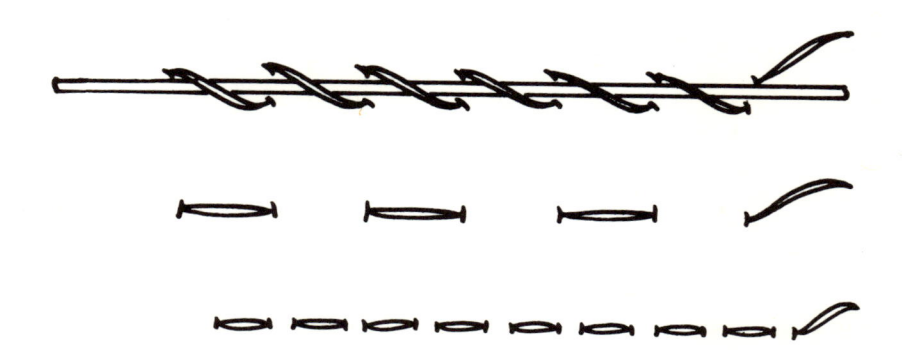

PAINT:

Poster paint or latex house paint will give excellent results for all costumes. Watercolors are successful on small areas. The colors specified are only suggestions. Use colors or any combinations that are pleasing to you.

GLUE:

The white household glues such as Elmer's Glue-All, LePage's White Glue, and Solomon's Sobo Glue are the most satisfactory. They are easy to apply, safe to use, and dry fast. Apply directly from the bottle or with a brush.

6

POSTER BOARD, CARDBOARD, AND PAPER:

Poster board usually comes in sheets 22 inches by 28 inches in a variety of colors. Cardboard cartons obtained from grocery stores are excellent when heavy cardboard is needed. Cardboard from writing tablets, shirt boards, and large cereal boxes is fine for small areas. Construction paper is satisfactory for most costumes. If a shiny surface is needed, use shelf paper. Do experiment with various kinds of paper available. Newspaper is excellent for making patterns. For crepe paper, sheets are preferable to streamers because the paper can be cut in different widths.

MEASUREMENTS:

All dimensions are given with width first and height or length second.

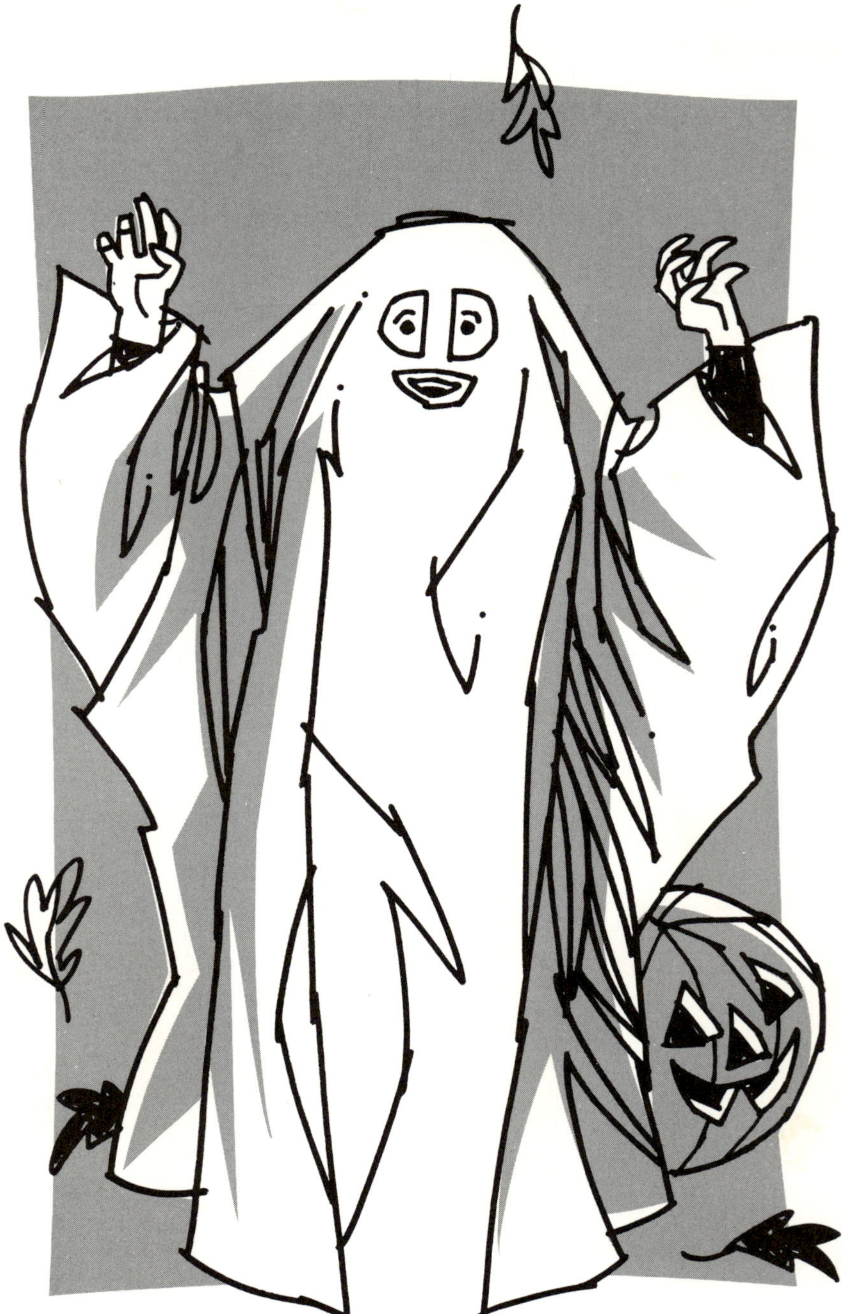

GHOST

MATERIALS:
piece of old white sheet
    twice as long as your height
    and as wide as the distance
    between your fingertips
    with arms stretched out

TOOLS:
tape measure
scissors
needle and
    white thread
pencil

STEPS:

1. Fold the sheet crosswise wrong side out. Sew each of the sides together (Figure 1). Turn inside out.

2. In the center of the costume, about 4 inches down from the top fold, draw big eyes and a mouth and cut them out of the front part of the costume. Near the top corners cut slits large enough for arms to come through (Figure 2).

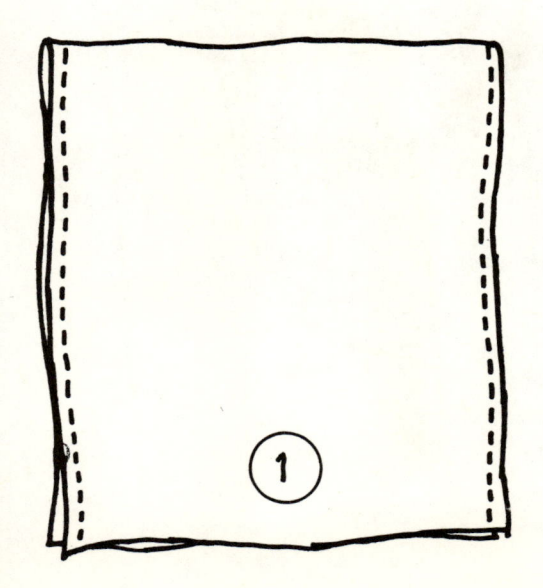

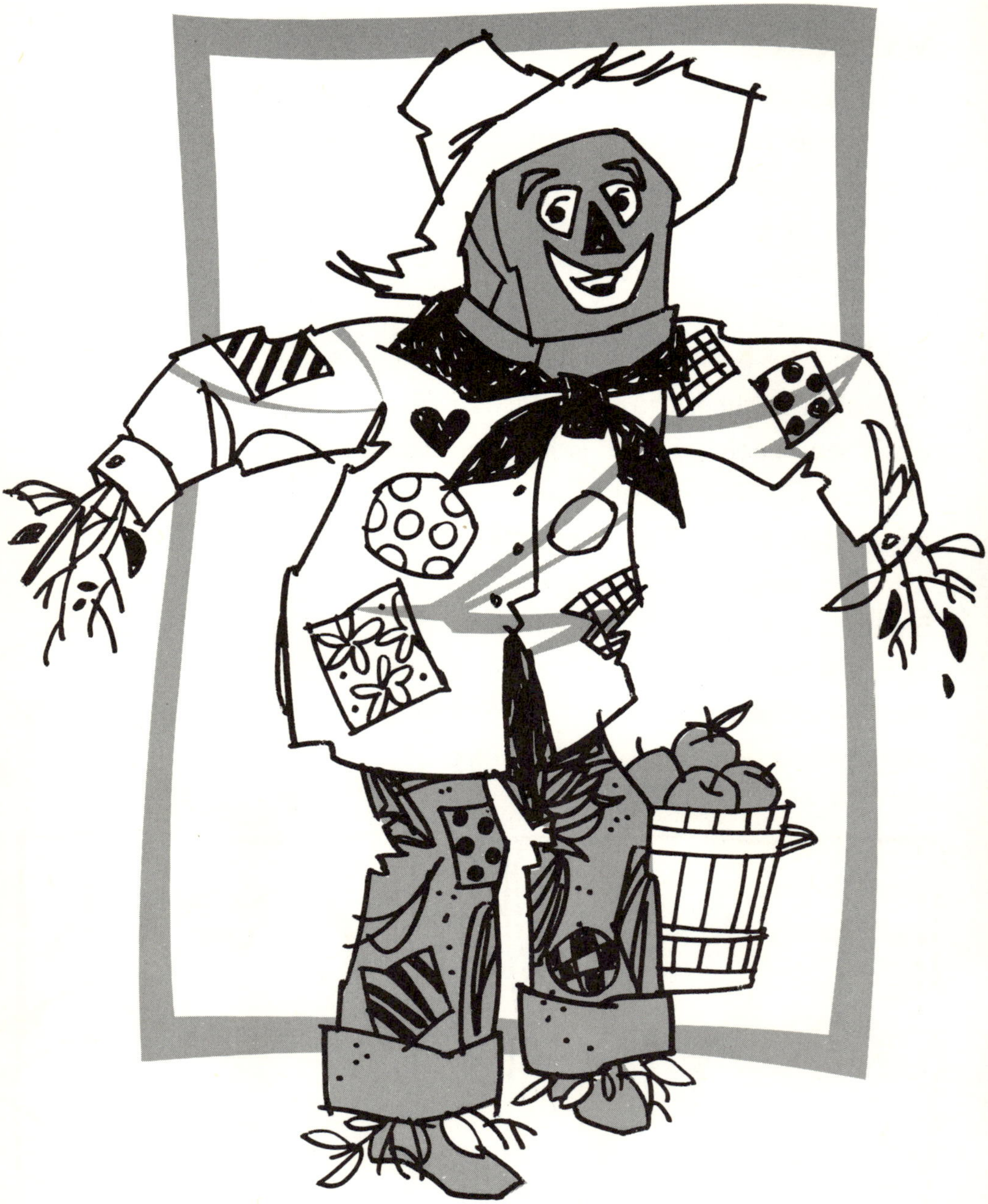

SCARECROW

MATERIALS:
large-sized pajama top or shirt
   with sleeves that cover your hands
jeans
scarf
straw hat
paper bag large enough to fit
   comfortably over your head
scraps of bright material
dried weeds, twigs, or
   strips of crepe paper
cellophane or masking tape

TOOLS:
black crayon
scissors
needle and thread

STEPS:

1. Fold top of paper bag down about an inch. Put the bag over your head, and, with a crayon, mark the locations of your eyes and mouth. Remove bag, draw eyes and mouth, and cut out. Outline eye and mouth holes with crayon, and draw eyebrows and nose (Figure 1).

2. Cut patches from scraps of material and sew them on shirt and jeans.

3. Tape or sew dried weeds, twigs, or strips of crepe paper just inside the shirt sleeves. Tape weeds to the tops of your shoes (Figure 2).

4. Wear the paper bag over your head together with jeans, shirt, scarf, and hat.

②

LONGHORN STEER

MATERIALS:
dark-colored blanket
paper bag large enough to fit
    comfortably over your head
another paper bag of any size
household glue
white cardboard,
    20 inches by 9 inches
3 strips dark material,
    each 1 inch by 1 yard

TOOLS:
black felt-tip
    marker or crayon
scissors
ruler
safety pins

STEPS:

1. Put the large paper bag over your head, and, with a crayon, mark the location of your eyes. Remove bag. Draw eyes and cut out. Draw a steer's face on the bag (Figure 1). Draw ears on the other bag (Figure 2). Outline face and ears with marker or crayon. Cut out and glue ears to the head just above the eyes.

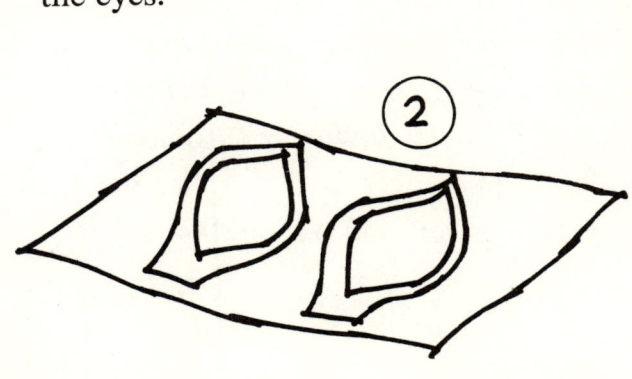

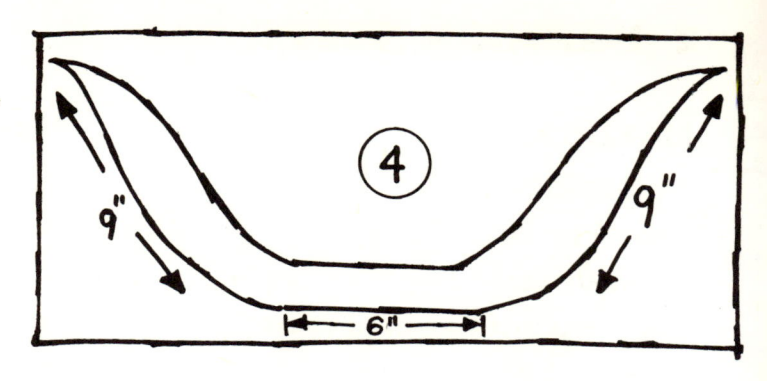

2. Cut a perpendicular slit, 1½ inches long, on each side of the head at fold of the bag (Figure 3).

3. On white cardboard, draw two curved horns each 9 inches long and 1 inch wide, joined together by a straight section 6 inches long (Figure 4). Cut the horns out and put through the slits.

4. For the tail, braid three strips of material together to about 3 inches from the end, and tie the end off. Cut narrow slits in the end of the tail and fluff out (Figure 5).

5. Two people are needed to be the steer's body. Both bend over in the same direction. The front person wears the steer's head. The person behind him keeps his head down. Have someone put the blanket over both people, pin the ends together, and pin on the tail.

14

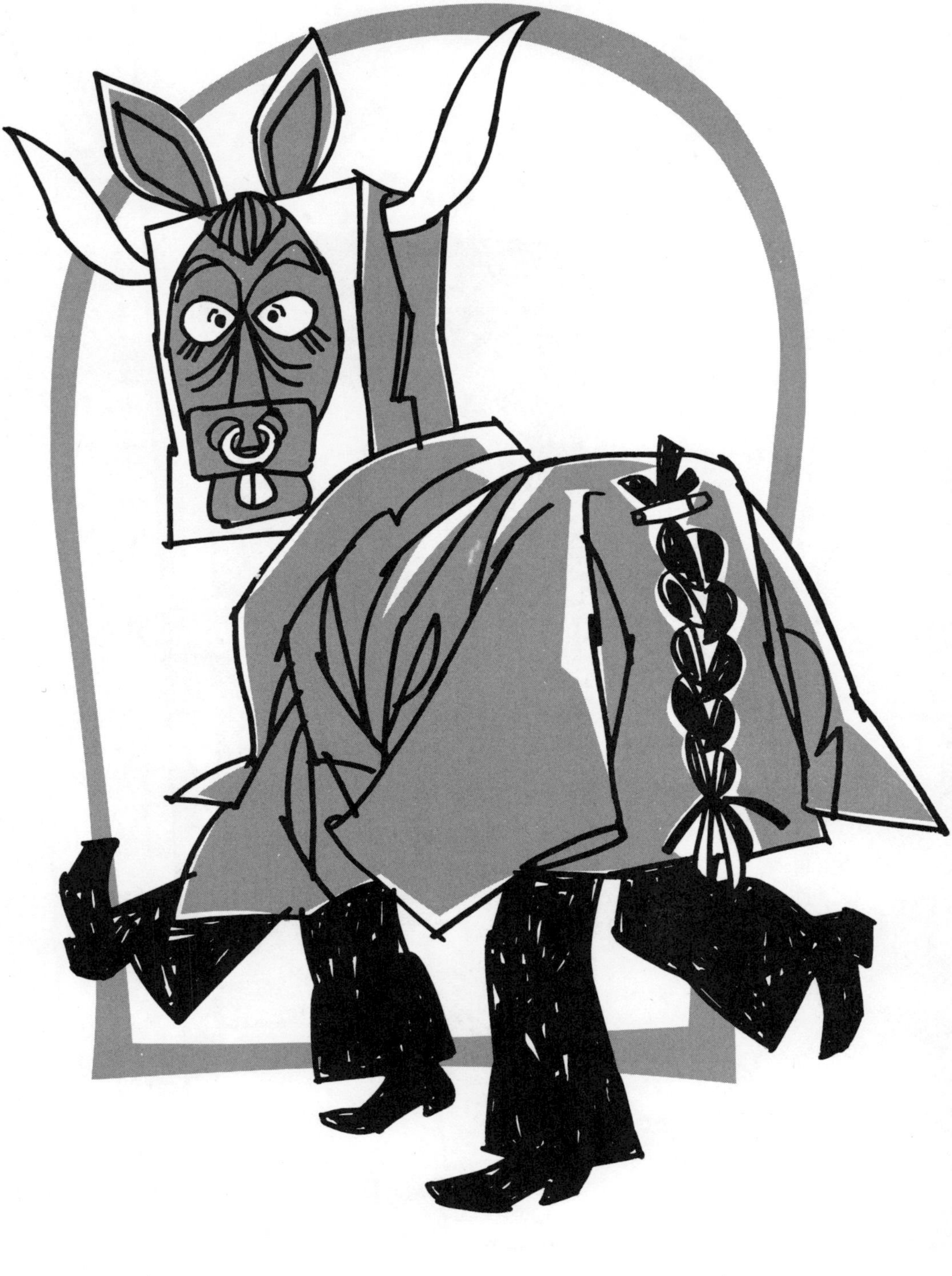

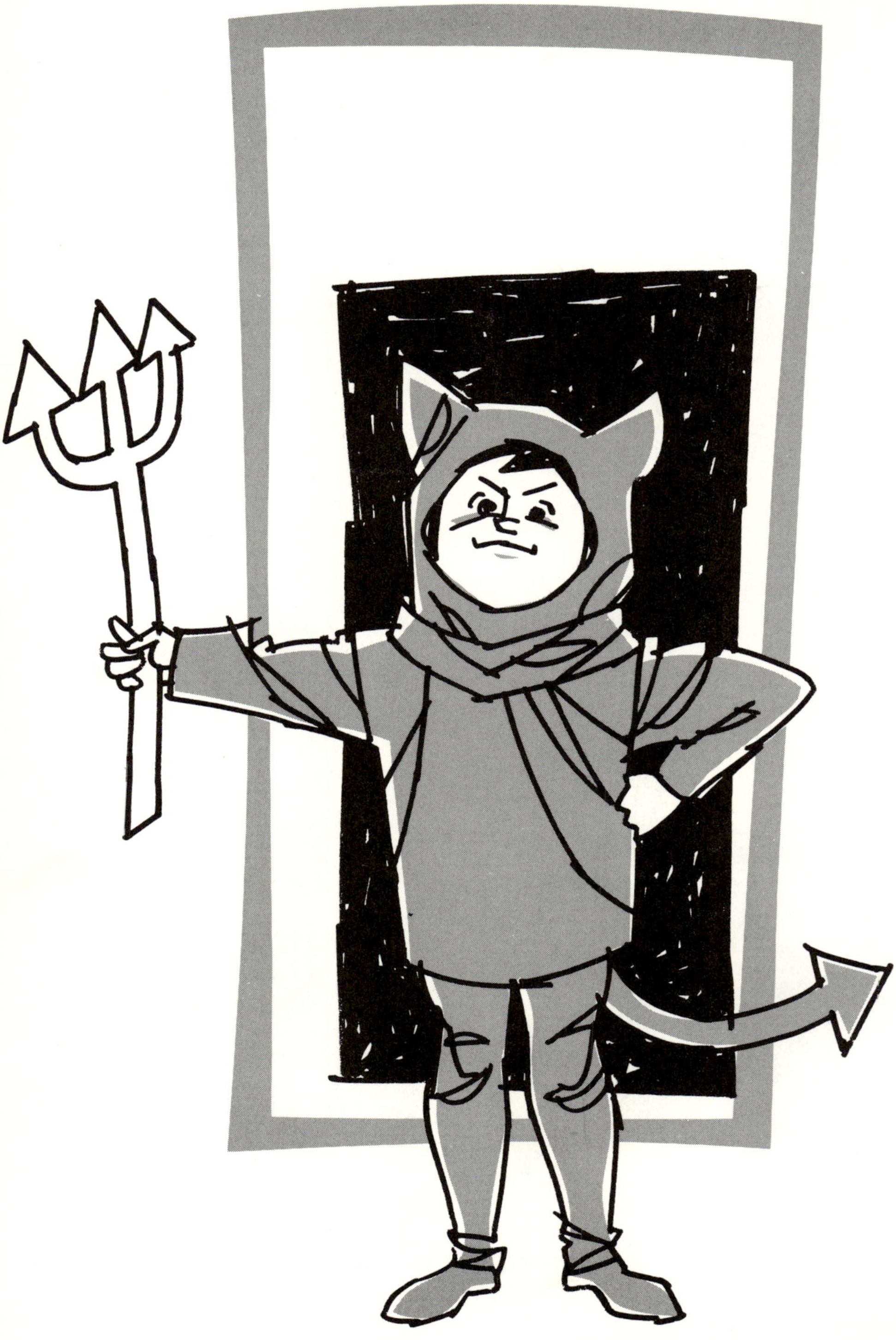

DEVIL

MATERIALS:

red leotards or
   red pants and long-sleeved sweater
piece of red material,
   26 inches by 19 inches
red cardboard or
   white cardboard painted red,
   11 inches by 28 inches

TOOLS:

newspapers
pencil
ruler
scissors
straight pins
needle and
   red thread
safety pin

STEPS:

1. Fold a newspaper and draw a pattern for the front of the hood (Figure 1). Fold another newspaper and draw a pattern for the back of the hood (Figure 2). Cut out both patterns.

2. Cut material into two pieces, each

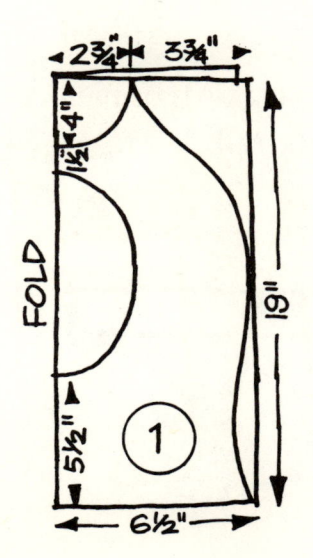

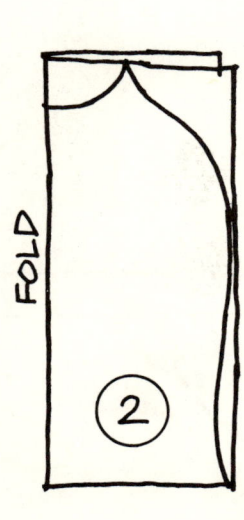

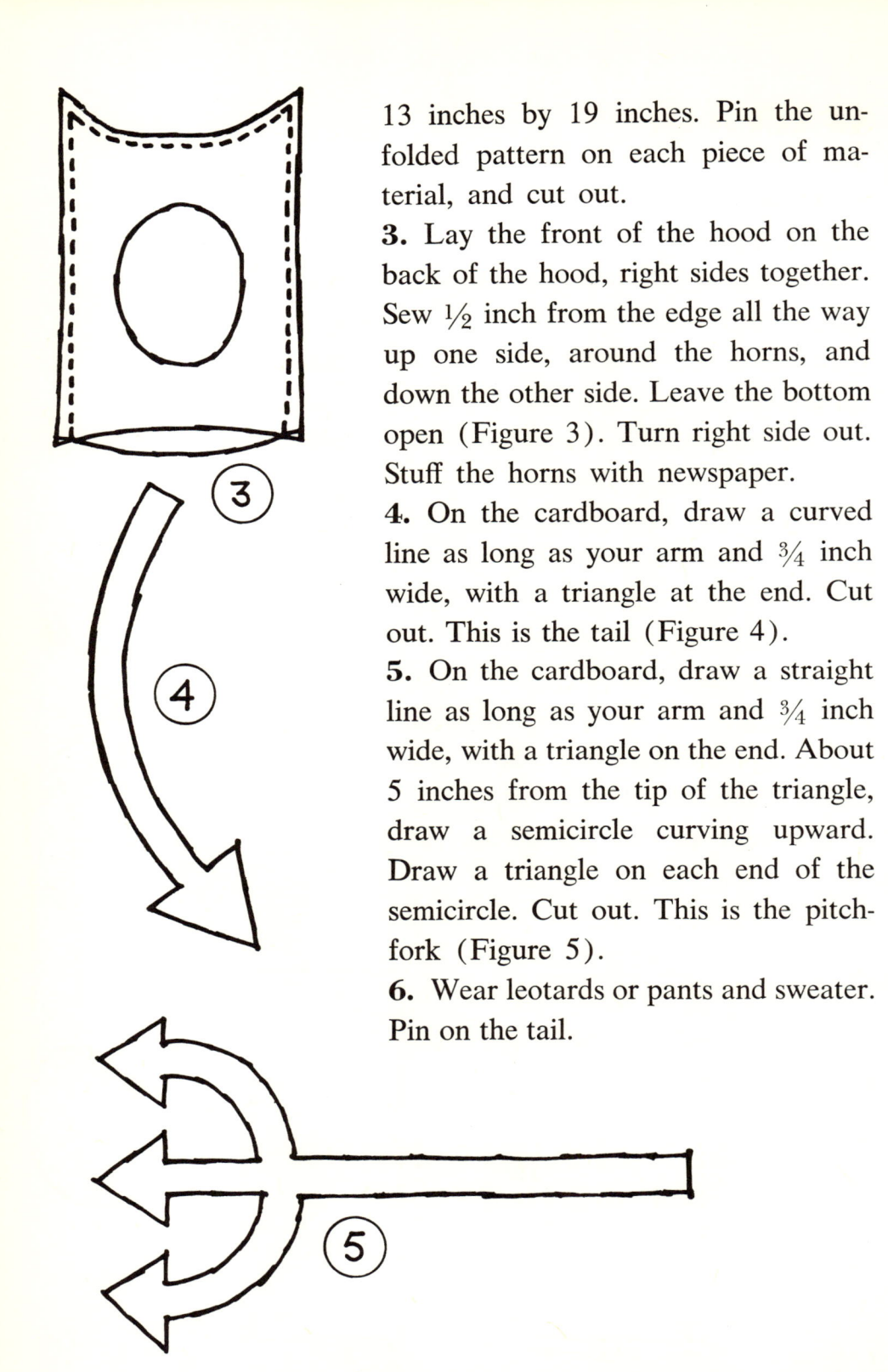

13 inches by 19 inches. Pin the unfolded pattern on each piece of material, and cut out.

3. Lay the front of the hood on the back of the hood, right sides together. Sew ½ inch from the edge all the way up one side, around the horns, and down the other side. Leave the bottom open (Figure 3). Turn right side out. Stuff the horns with newspaper.

4. On the cardboard, draw a curved line as long as your arm and ¾ inch wide, with a triangle at the end. Cut out. This is the tail (Figure 4).

5. On the cardboard, draw a straight line as long as your arm and ¾ inch wide, with a triangle on the end. About 5 inches from the tip of the triangle, draw a semicircle curving upward. Draw a triangle on each end of the semicircle. Cut out. This is the pitchfork (Figure 5).

6. Wear leotards or pants and sweater. Pin on the tail.

SPACEMAN

MATERIALS:
long-sleeved pajamas or
    jeans and shirt
gloves
pair large socks
paper bag large enough to fit
    comfortably over your head
2 square or rectangular boxes
    (such as soup mix or cake mix)
twine
cellophane tape
bright-colored paint
household glue
2 round cereal boxes
    (such as oatmeal)
2 pipe cleaners

TOOLS:
scissors
ruler
pencil
paintbrush

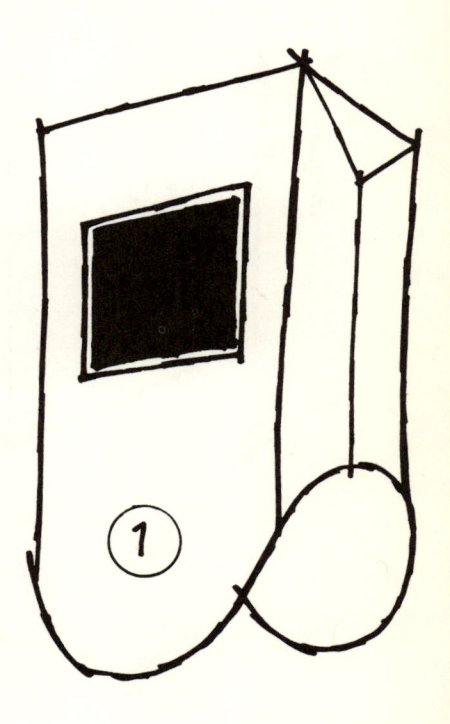

STEPS:

1. Cut the top front and back of the bag in a concave curve and the sides in an opposite curve. Cut a hole 4½ inches wide and 4½ inches high in the center front of the bag. This is the helmet (Figure 1).

2. In the center of the narrow sides of each square or rectangular box make a

19

small hole. Draw a 28-inch piece of twine through the two holes of each box. Then make two holes 2 inches apart in the top of each box. Draw another 28-inch piece of twine through one hole and out the other (Figure 2). Tape the tops of the boxes shut. One box is the radio transmitter. The other box is the radio receiver.

3. Paint the outsides of all four boxes and the helmet a bright color. Let the paint dry.

4. Glue the two round boxes—the air tanks—side by side to the radio receiver (Figure 3).

5. Twist the ends of two pipe cleaners

20

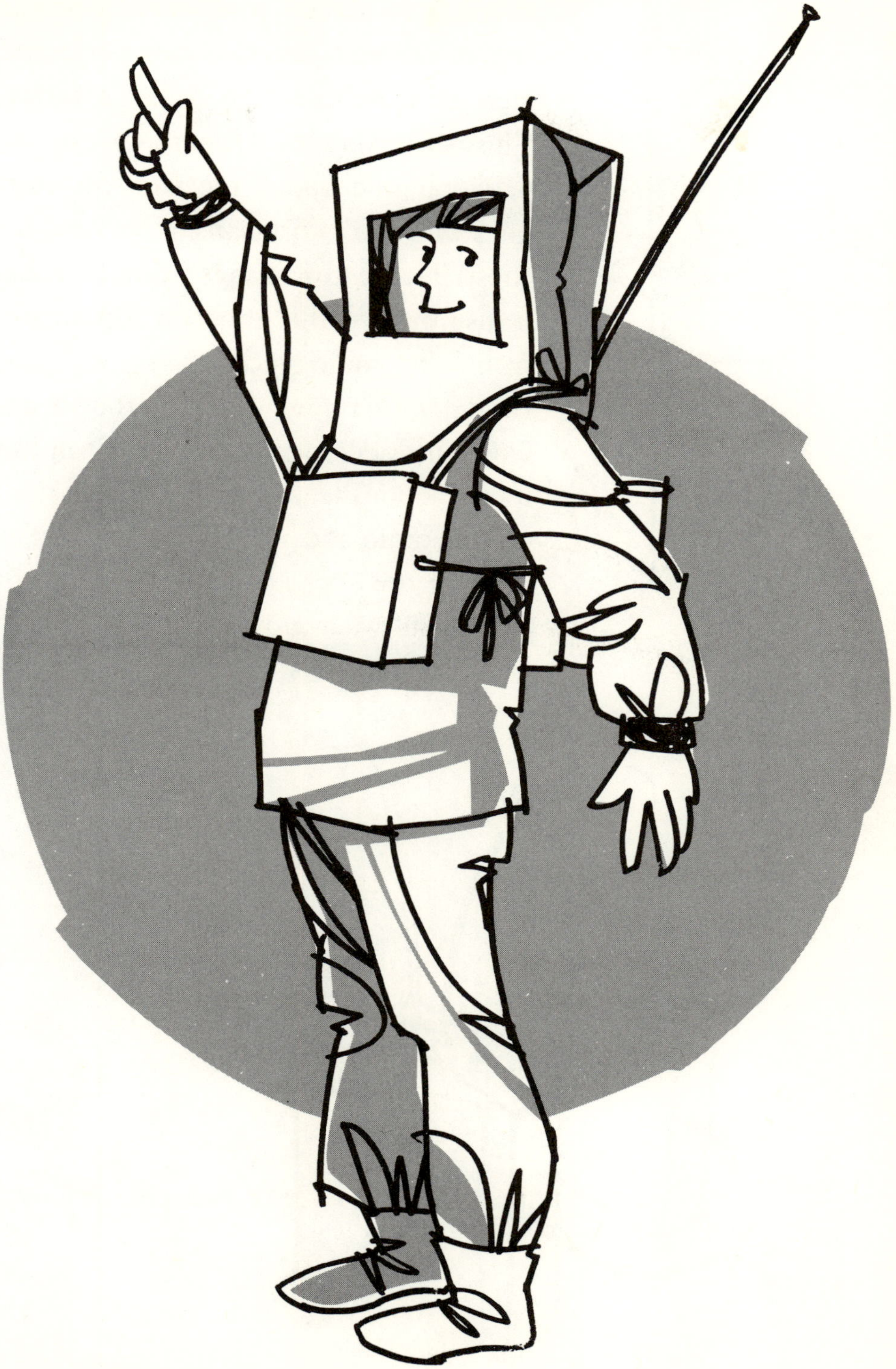

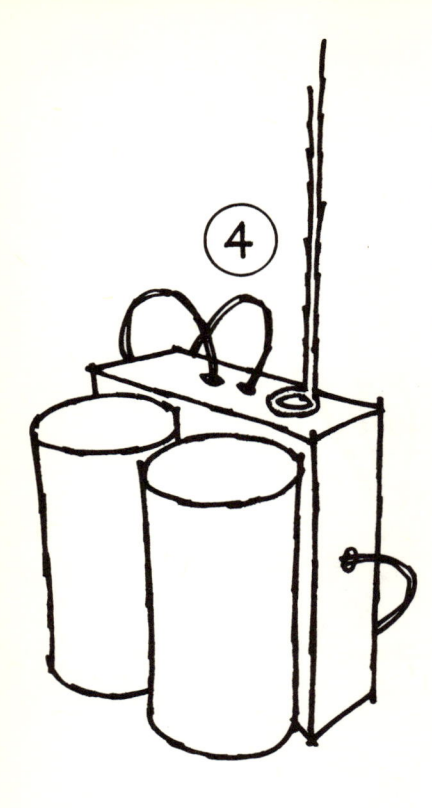

together to make a long one. Bend one end of the stem into a small circle and glue it to the top of the radio receiver. This is the antenna (Figure 4).

6. Wear the radio receiver on your back and the radio transmitter on your chest. Tie the top strings from the radio transmitter to the opposite top strings from the radio receiver across your shoulders. At your waist, tie the strings from the sides of the radio transmitter to the opposite strings from the sides of the radio receiver (Figure 5).

7. Pull the socks up over pajamas or jeans, and wear gloves.

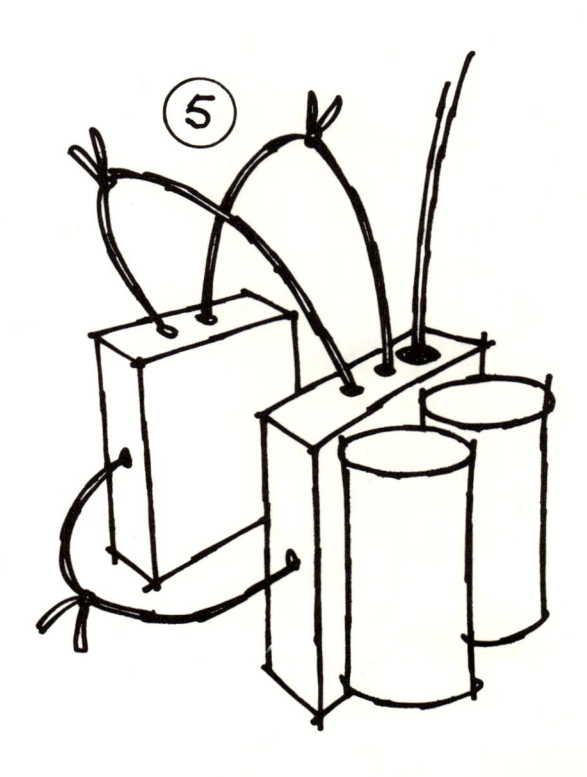

OCTOPUS

MATERIALS:
black leotards or
   black pants and long-sleeved shirt
commercial ice-cream container or
   any round cardboard box
   that will fit comfortably
   over your head and reach
   to your shoulders
black paint
piece of white construction paper
piece of black construction paper
household glue
white paint
black bath towel or
   black material of equal size
newspapers
masking tape

TOOLS:
paintbrush
pencil
scissors
ruler
needle and
   black thread
   or stapler

STEPS:

1. Paint the container black. Let the paint dry.

2. Draw two large eyes on the white paper about half the height of the container, and cut out. On the black paper, draw two smaller circles; cut out and glue a circle near the bottom of each eye. Draw a circle about the size of a pop-bottle cap in the center of the black part of each eye, and cut out. On the white paper, draw and cut out an oval-shaped nose.

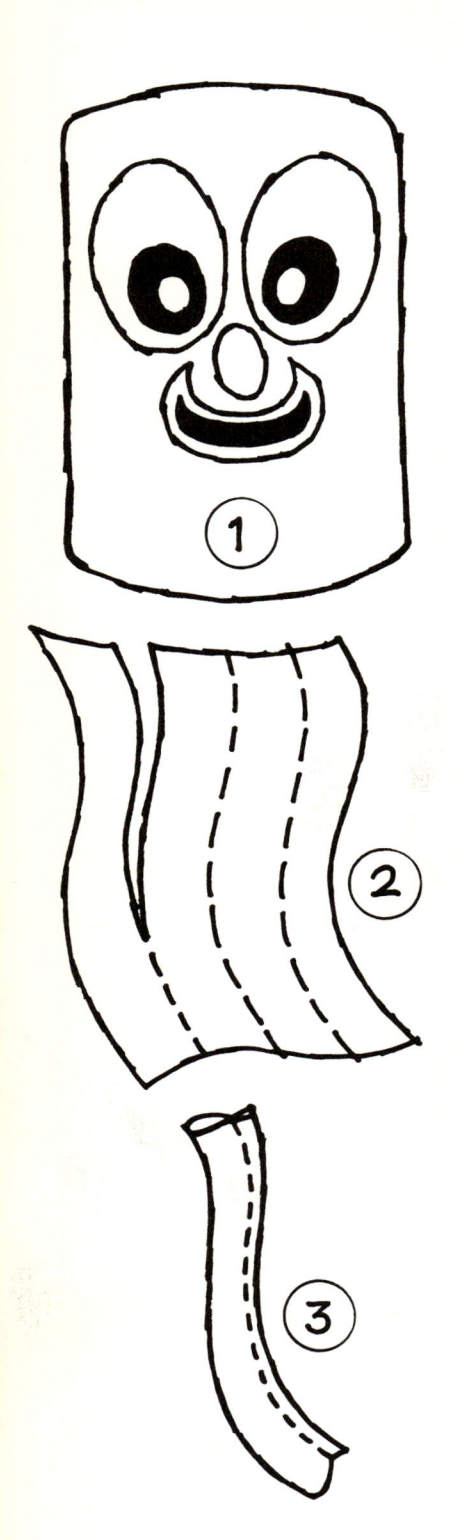

3. Hold the container on one shoulder against the side of your face and have someone mark the places for your eyes. Cut out eyeholes about the size of a pop-bottle cap. Glue on the paper eyes, being certain the holes line up with those in the container. Glue on nose. Cut a mouth opening and outline it in white paint (Figure 1).

4. Cut the towel lengthwise in four equal strips (Figure 2). Sew or staple together the sides of each strip to make tentacles (Figure 3). Stuff lightly with crushed newspaper. Tape an end of each tentacle halfway up inside the container, placing two at the front and two at the back. Tape the tentacles in several places to hold them firmly to the container.

5. Wear with black leotards or black pants and long-sleeved shirt. Your arms and legs are the other four tentacles.

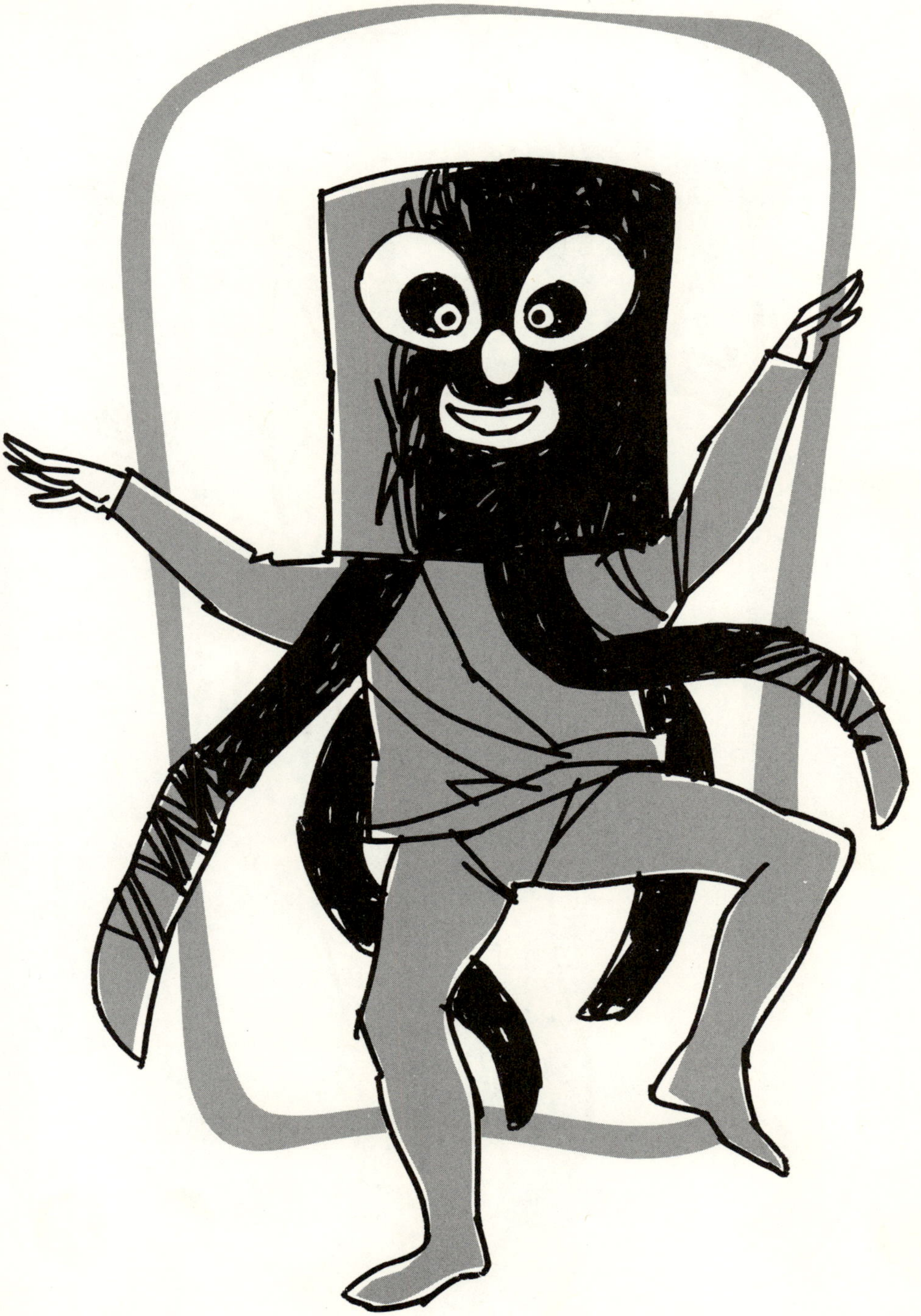

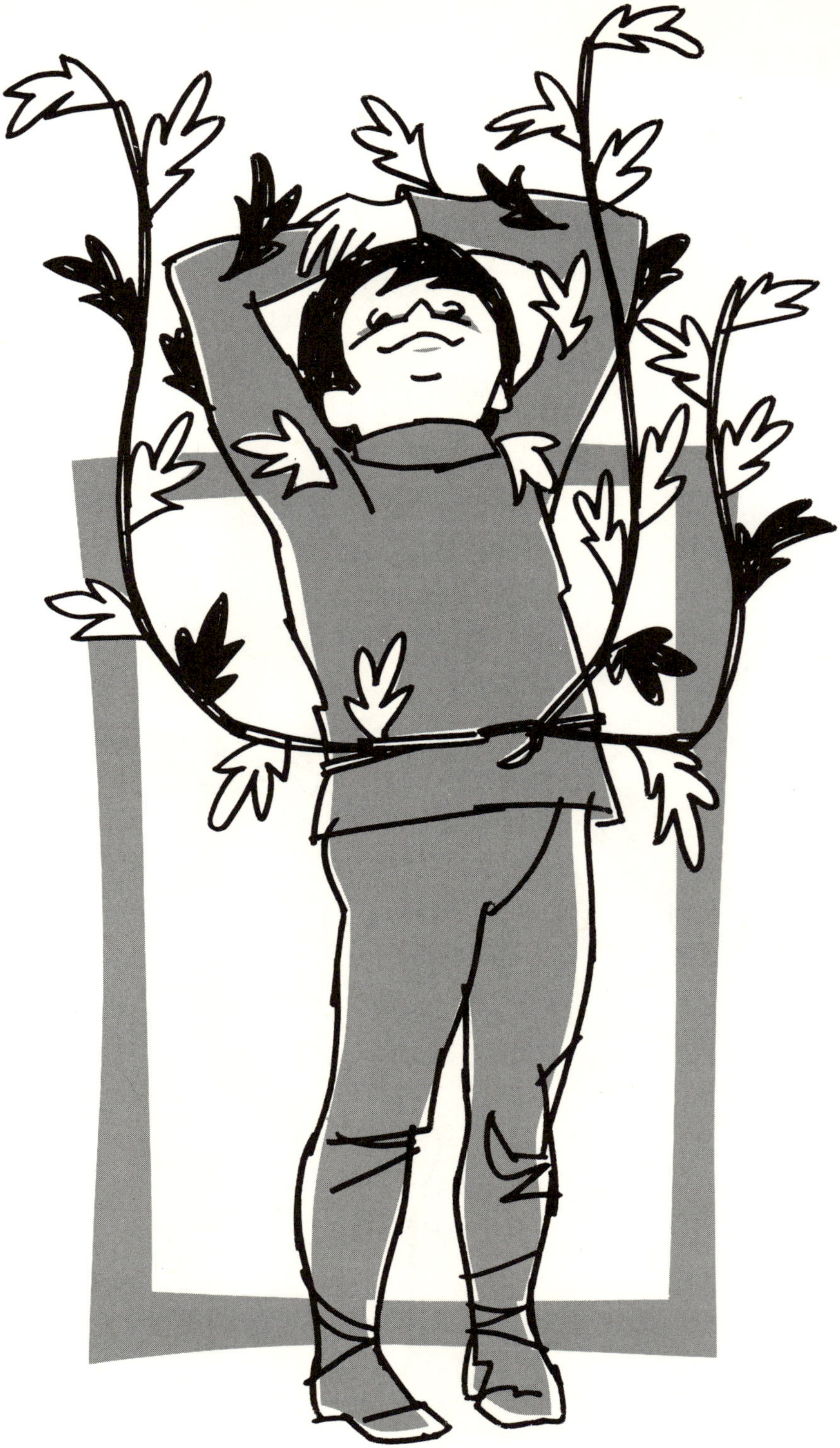

TREE

MATERIALS:

brown leotards or
  long-sleeved brown shirt and pants
11½ feet of 9-gauge aluminum wire
masking tape
1/3 package brown crepe paper
yellow, orange, red, and green
  construction paper
twister fasteners
cellophane tape

TOOLS:

pliers or
  wire cutter
scissors
pencil
ruler
piece of cardboard

STEPS:

1. With pliers or wire cutter, cut the wire in half. Cover all four ends with several layers of masking tape.

2. Cut strips of crepe paper crosswise about 1 inch wide. Starting at one end of the wire, wrap the crepe paper around the entire length of both pieces of wire (Figure 1). When you come to the end of a paper strip, join it to another strip with tape.

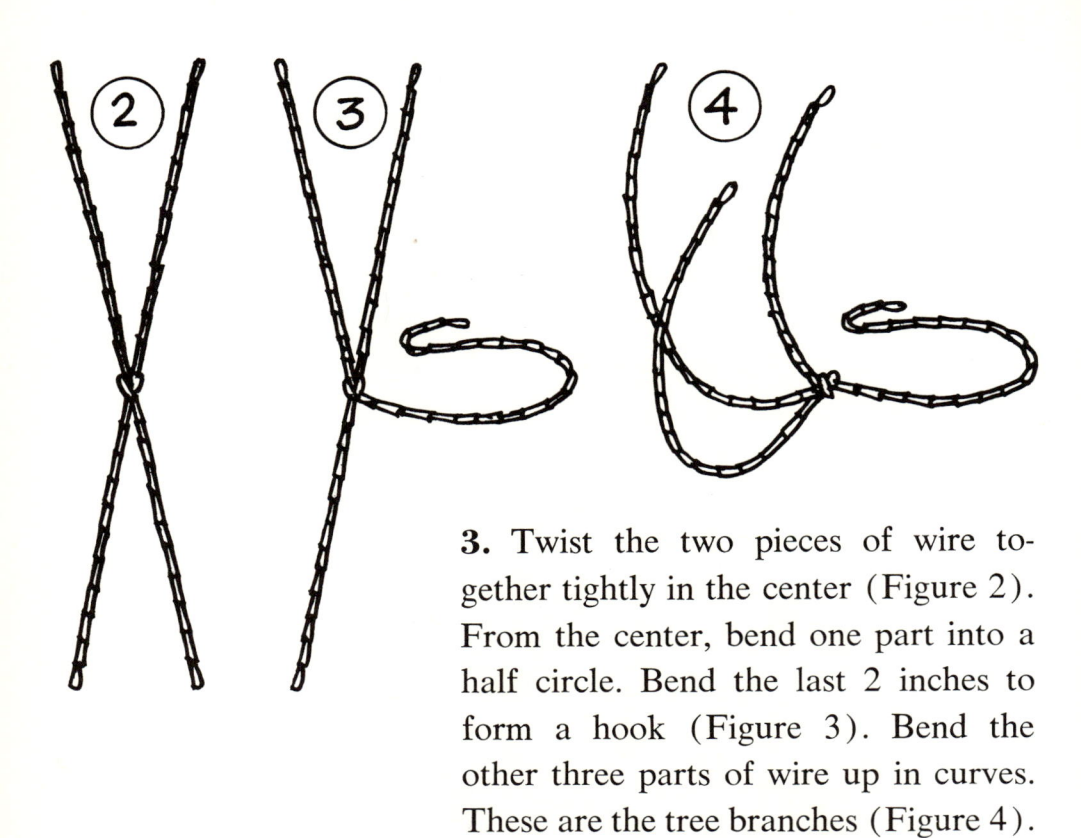

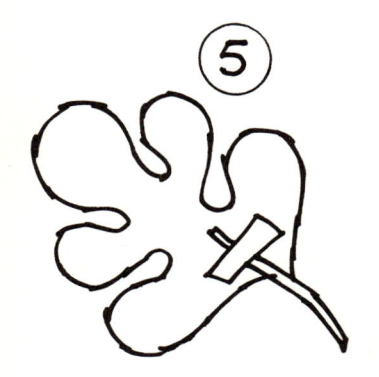

3. Twist the two pieces of wire together tightly in the center (Figure 2). From the center, bend one part into a half circle. Bend the last 2 inches to form a hook (Figure 3). Bend the other three parts of wire up in curves. These are the tree branches (Figure 4).

4. On a piece of cardboard draw a leaf shape about the size of your hand, and cut out. Using this as a pattern, cut about forty leaves from construction paper of different colors. Tape a twister fastener on the back of the leaves, with the twister extending an inch below the leaf (Figure 5). Twist the leaves tightly around the three branches so some stand straight up and others hang down.

28

5. With the branches in front of you, place the half circle of wire around your waist and hook it over the lower part of a branch (Figure 6).

6. Wear with brown leotards or brown shirt and pants. Tape several leaves on your shirt sleeves, and hold your arms up as branches.

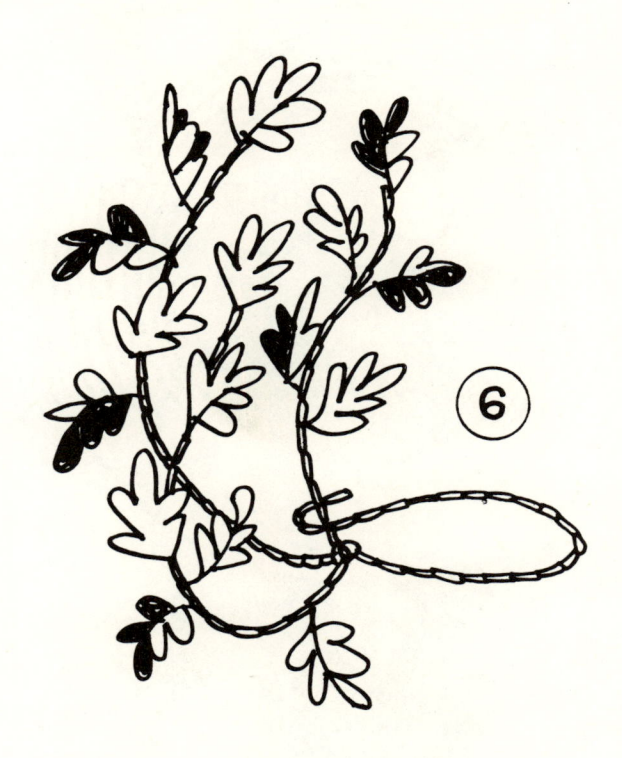

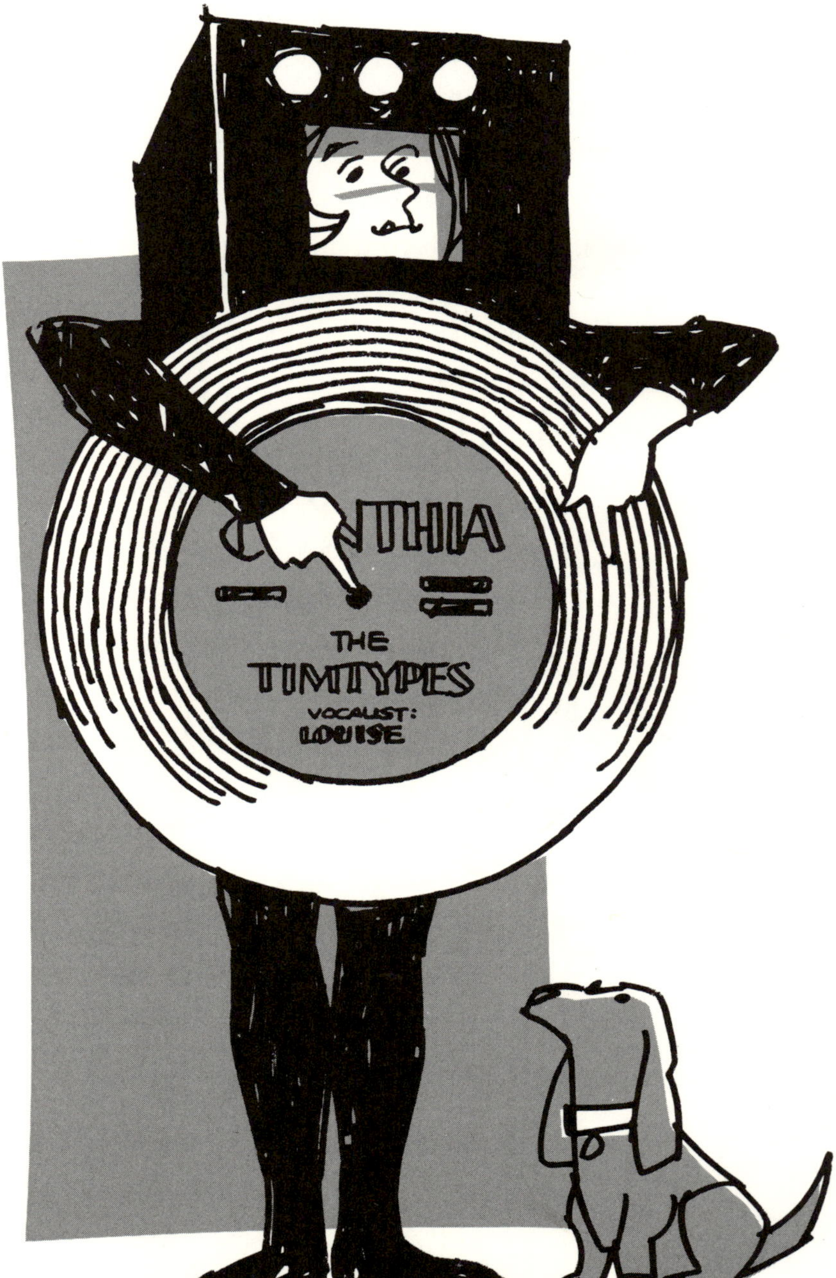
THE
TIMTYPES
VOCALIST:
LOUISE

RECORD PLAYER

MATERIALS:
black leotards or
    black long-sleeved shirt, pants,
    and shoes
cardboard box large enough to fit
    comfortably over your body and
    to reach from the top of your head
    to middle of your thighs
circle, 22 inches in diameter,
    cut out of cardboard
black paint
red shelf paper
black construction paper
household glue
white paint
3 small white plastic lids or
    3 circles of white paper
    about 1 inch in diameter

TOOLS:
scissors
pencil
ruler
paintbrush
    about 1 inch
    wide
black felt-tip
    marker

STEPS:

1. Cut the lid and flaps off the box. Hold the box with the bottom even with the top of your head. Have someone mark the places on the sides of the box where your arms will come through. Cut out armholes about 6 inches square. Put the box on your head and have someone mark a line even with your eyes. Take off the box and cut an opening about 4 inches high and 4 inches wide for your eyes, nose, and mouth. The box is the record-player speaker (Figure 1).

2. Paint the box and the round piece of cardboard black. Let the paint dry. Clean the brush thoroughly.

3. Cut a circle about 13 inches in diameter from the red paper and a circle 3 inches in diameter from the black paper. Glue the red circle in the center of the large cardboard circle. Glue the small black circle in the center of the red circle. With a marker, write the name of a record and a singing group on the red circle (Figure 2).

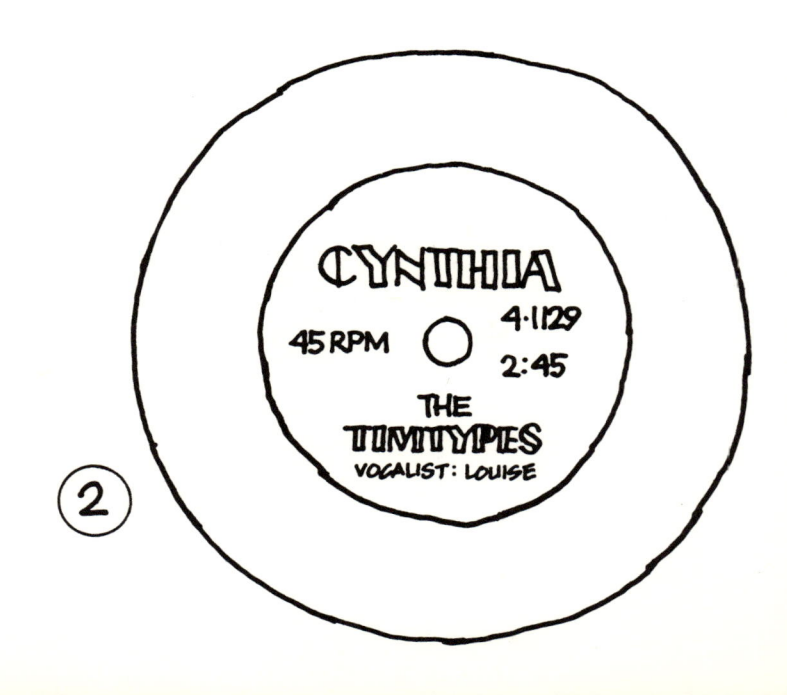

CYNTHIA

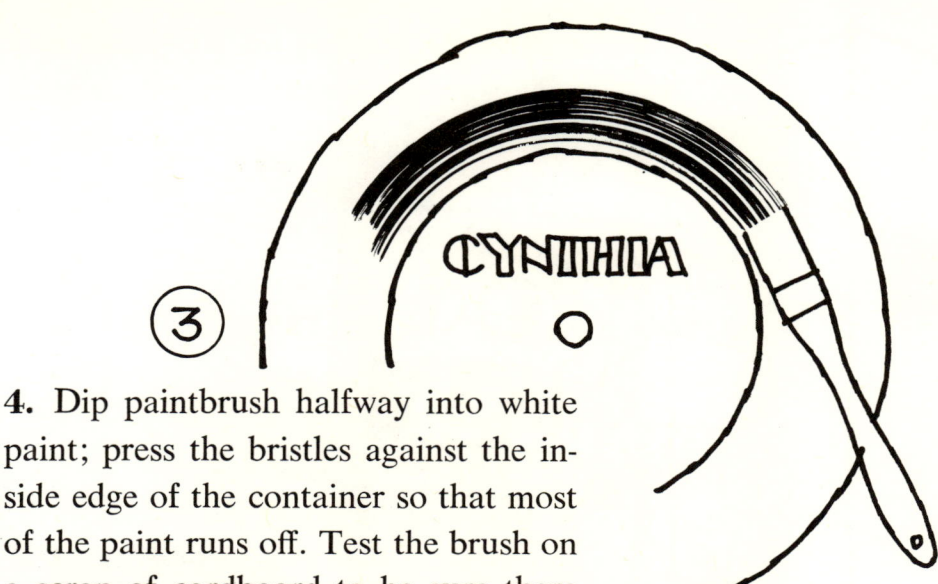

③

4. Dip paintbrush halfway into white paint; press the bristles against the inside edge of the container so that most of the paint runs off. Test the brush on a scrap of cardboard to be sure there is just enough paint on bristles to make "grooves" on the record. Starting from the outside edge of the black cardboard circle, brush around and around to the edge of the red circle (Figure 3). Let the paint dry.

5. Glue the record on the front of the box below the face opening. Glue the three plastic lids or the circles of white paper near the top of the record player for knobs. Let the glue dry.

6. Wear with black leotards or black shirt, pants, and shoes. Your arms will be the needle arm and the record holder.

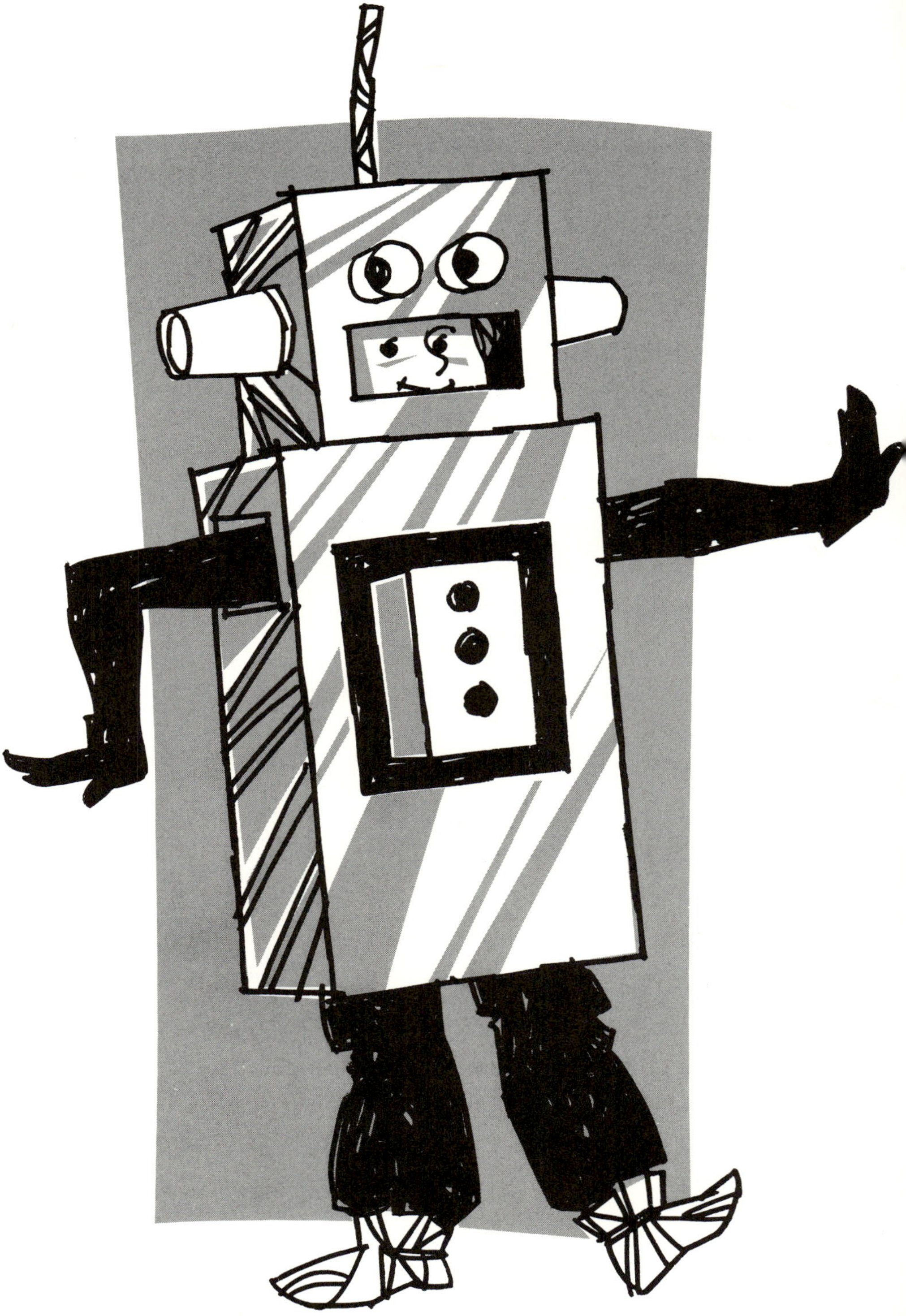

ROBOT

MATERIALS:
dark pants and long-sleeved shirt
dark gloves
cardboard box large enough to fit
   comfortably over your body and
   to reach from your shoulders
   to just above your knees
second cardboard box
   large enough to fit comfortably
   over your head and at least
   1/3 as high as the body box
third cardboard box
   about 6 inches by 8 inches
aluminum foil, 12 inches by 2 inches
cellophane tape
household glue
2 paper cups
2 cupcake liners
2 paper bags large enough
   to fit over your feet
silver paint
black construction paper
2 rubber bands

TOOLS:
scissors
pencil
ruler
paintbrush

STEPS:

1. Cut the lid and flaps off the biggest

box. Hold the box with the bottom even with your shoulders and have someone mark the places on the sides of the box where your arms will come through. Cut out armholes about 6 inches square. Cut a hole in the center bottom of the box big enough for your head to come through (Figure 1).

2. Cut the lid and flaps off the second box. Hold the box on one shoulder and have someone mark a line even with your eyes. At this level, cut an opening in the center of the box, 6 inches across and 1 inch high. This is the robot's mouth through which you will look (Figure 2).

3. Crush the foil into an antenna. Fold under an inch at one end and tape it to the center top of the head box. Glue a paper cup to each side of the head. Glue on cupcake liners for eyes (Figure 3).

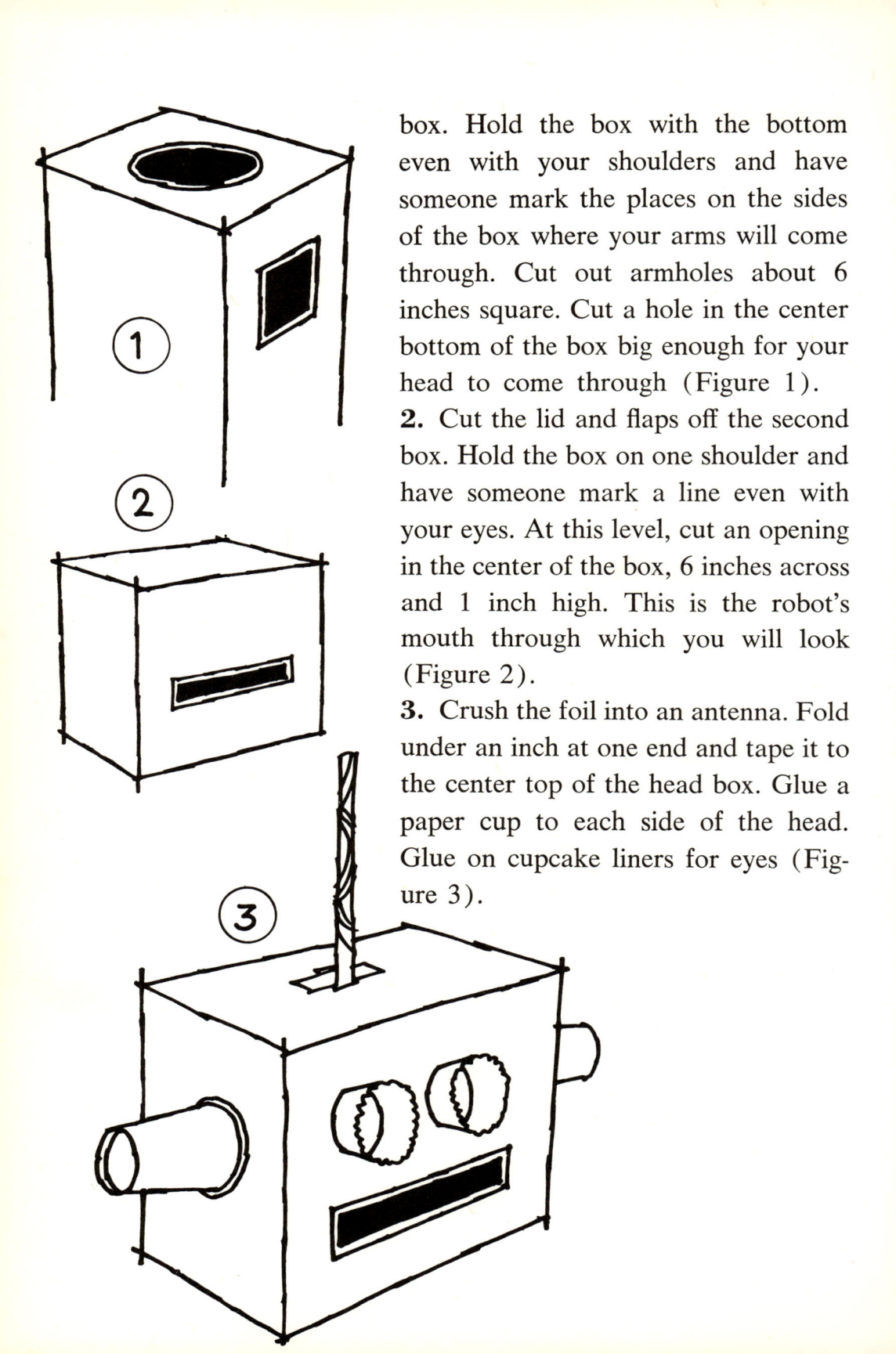

4. Paint all three boxes, paper cups, cupcake liners, and the two paper bags with silver paint. Let the paint dry.

5. Glue a piece of black paper, 8½ inches by 11 inches, to the center of the body, about 4 inches from the top. Glue the smallest box to the center of the black paper. This is the control box (Figure 4).

6. Cut out five circles of black paper the size of a quarter. Glue a circle inside each cupcake liner and three circles in a row on the control box.

7. Tape or glue head box to body box.

8. Wear robot costume over dark clothing. Fasten the paper bags on your feet with rubber bands.

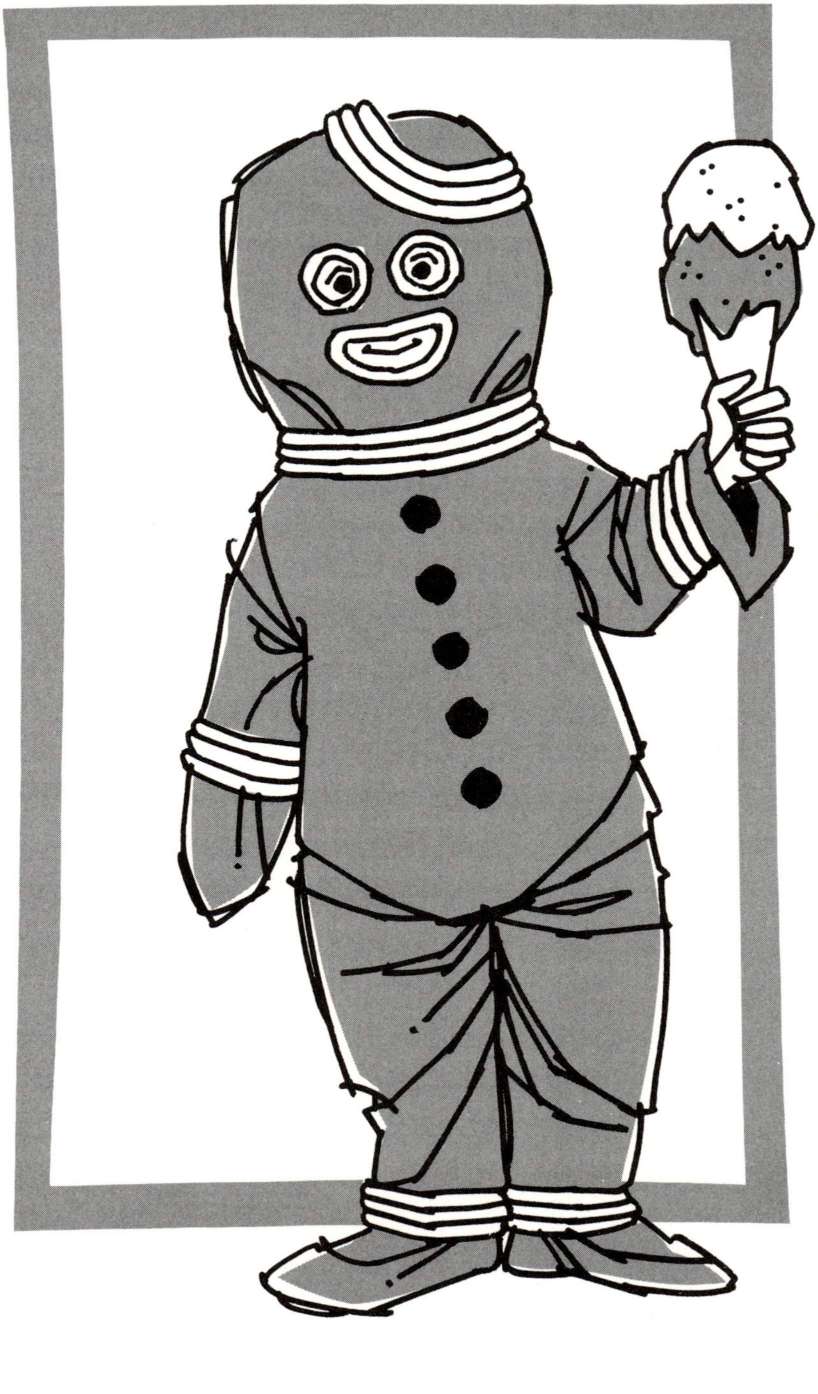

GINGERBREAD BOY

MATERIALS:

double-sized sheet, dyed brown,
    if you are under 3 feet 3 inches tall;
    2 double-sized sheets, dyed brown,
    if you are over 3 feet 3 inches
4 yards white piping cord
    as thick as your little finger
household glue
piece of white cardboard
piece of thin cardboard

TOOLS:

newspaper
cellophane tape
crayon
scissors
straight pins
needle and
    brown thread
pencil
aluminum foil
safety pins

STEPS:

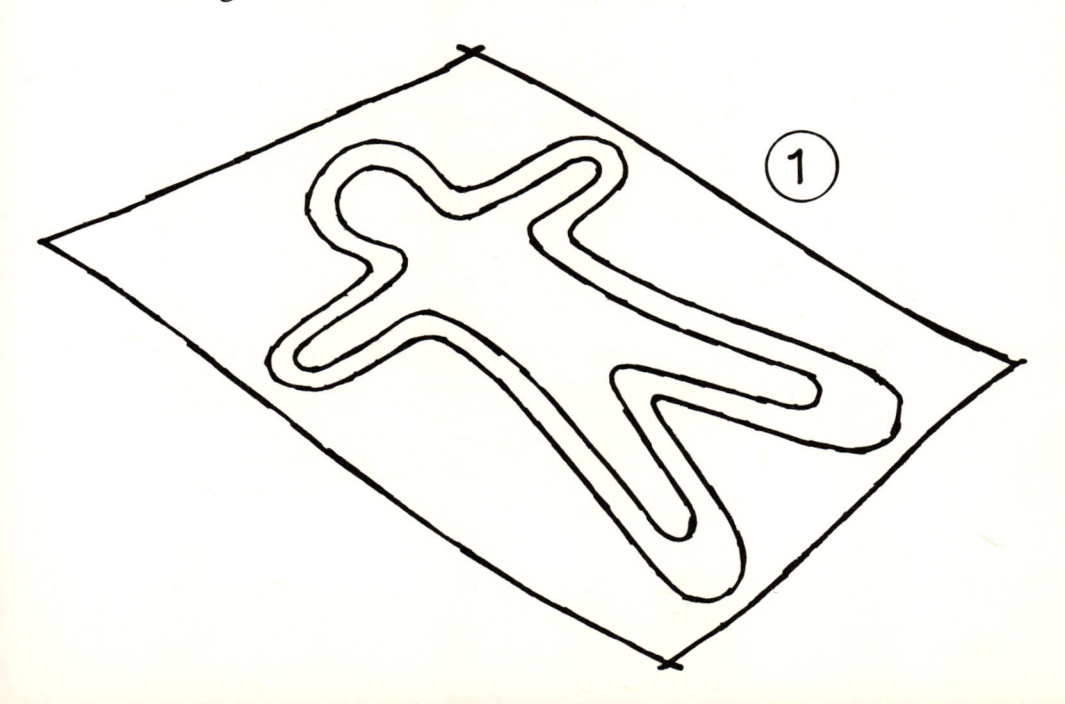

1. Spread newspapers on the floor. Tape the papers together where they join. Lie down on the papers with both arms straight out and have someone draw around you with a crayon (Figure 1). Then draw another line 3 inches outside of this line. Cut out the pattern.

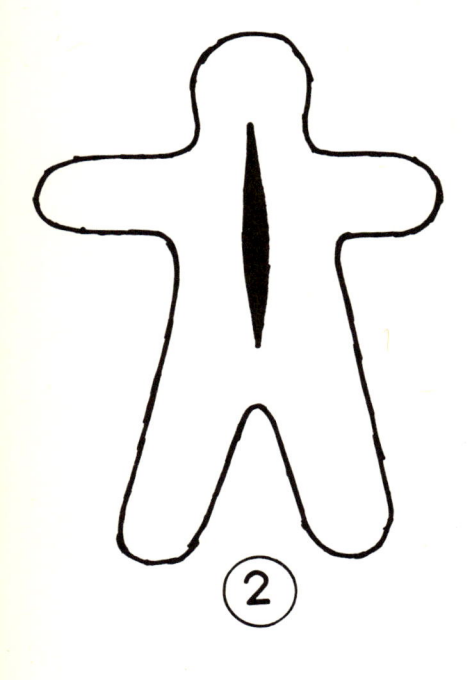

2. Fold the sheet crosswise, wrong side out, or put two sheets together, wrong sides out. Place on floor, pin on the pattern, and cut out. From the neck, cut down the center of the back of the costume about the length of your arm (Figure 2). Do not cut an opening in the front piece.

3. Pin the back and front together and sew ½ inch from the edge all the way around. Turn right side out.

4. Put the costume on. With a crayon, mark the places for your eyes and mouth. Take the costume off. Draw and cut out eye and mouth holes. At the inside of the wrists, cut 4-inch slits for hands to come through.

5. The cord will be the "frosting" on the gingerbread boy. Glue pieces on the front of the costume at neck, wrists, and ankles. On one side of the head, glue three pieces of cord for the hat. Glue cord ½ inch outside the eye and mouth holes. To keep glue from sticking to the back of the costume, put pieces of foil between the front and back at the places where you glue on the cord.

6. From white cardboard, cut five buttons the size of a quarter and glue on the center of the front.

7. Cut out a round piece of thin cardboard the size of your head. In the center, cut a hole large enough to encircle your eyes and mouth. Tape the cardboard to the inside front of the head (Figure 3).

8. Back of the costume should be pinned together when you wear it.

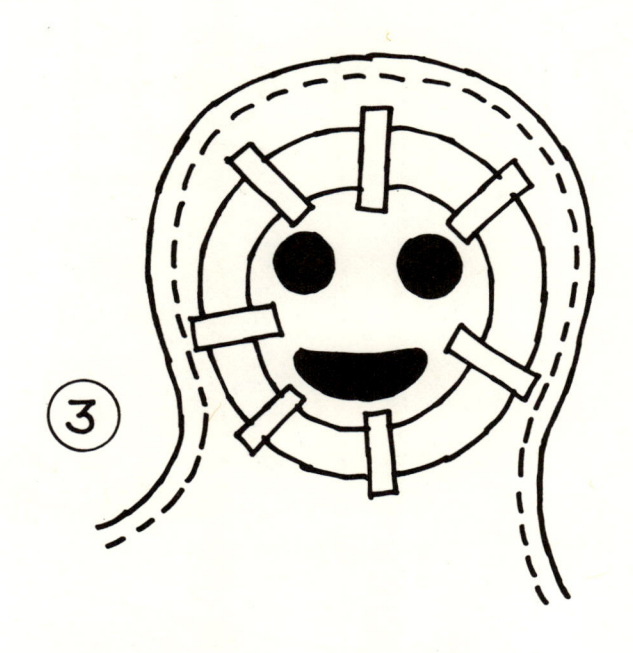

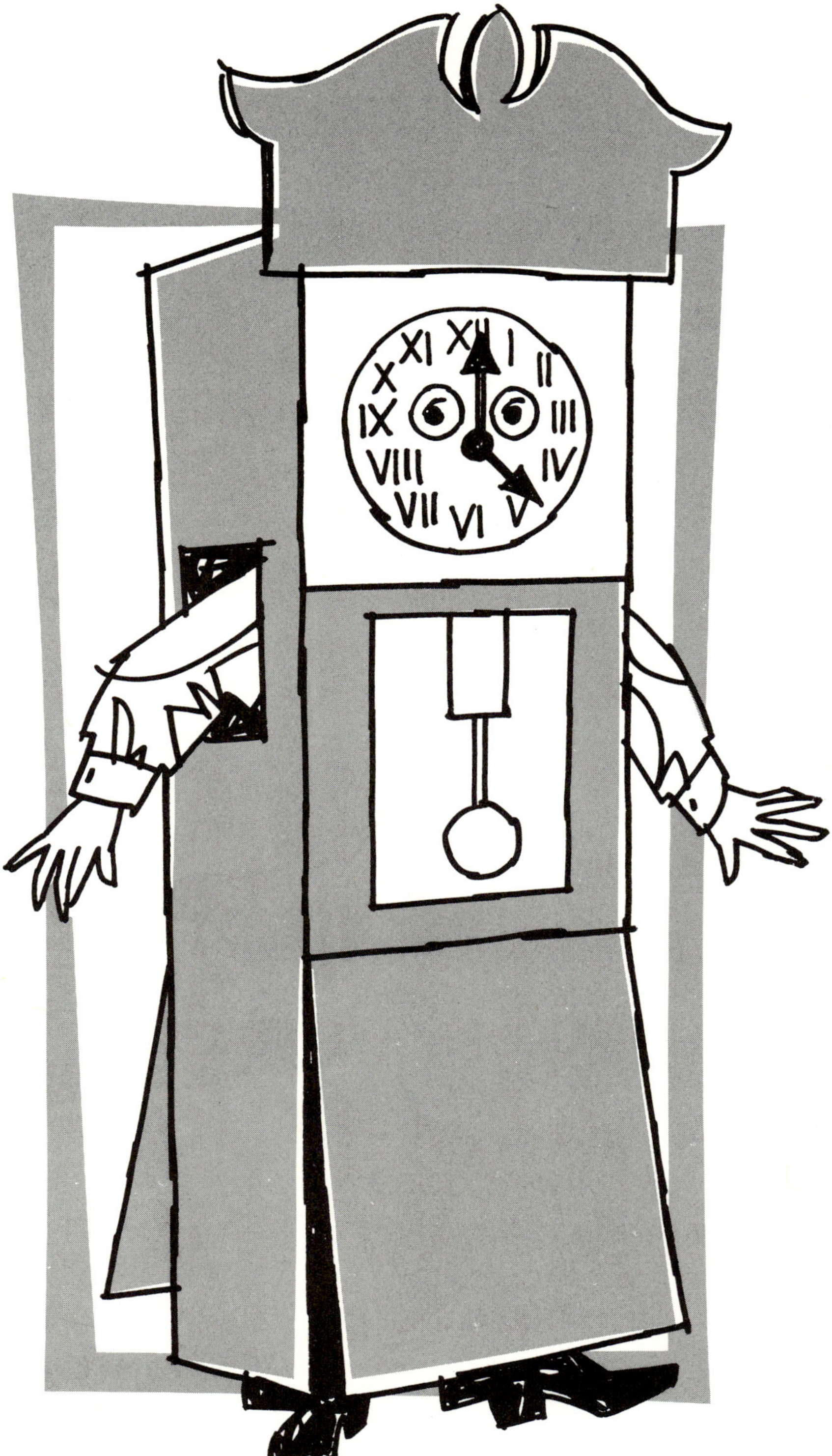

GRANDFATHER CLOCK

MATERIALS:

white or yellow long-sleeved shirt
cardboard box large enough to fit
    over your body comfortably
    and as long as your full height
cardboard
household glue
copper or brown paint
yellow poster board
white paper plate
black construction paper
white poster board

TOOLS:

scissors
pencil
ruler
paintbrush
black felt-tip
    marker or crayon

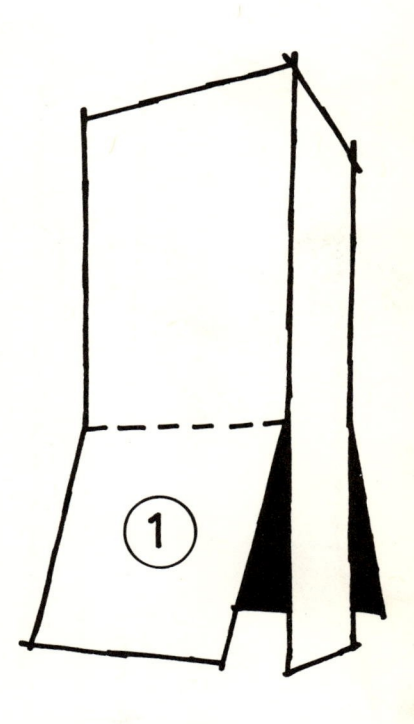

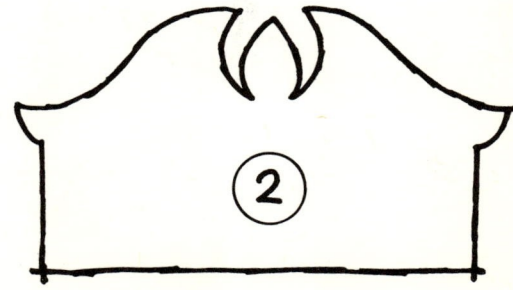

STEPS:

1. Cut the lid and flaps off the box. At the four corners of the open end, cut the box to a distance just above your knees. Bend the flaps out so you can walk within the box (Figure 1).

2. Cut a piece of cardboard 2 inches wider than the box and 12 inches high. Draw a scroll at the top and cut out (Figure 2). Spread glue on the bottom

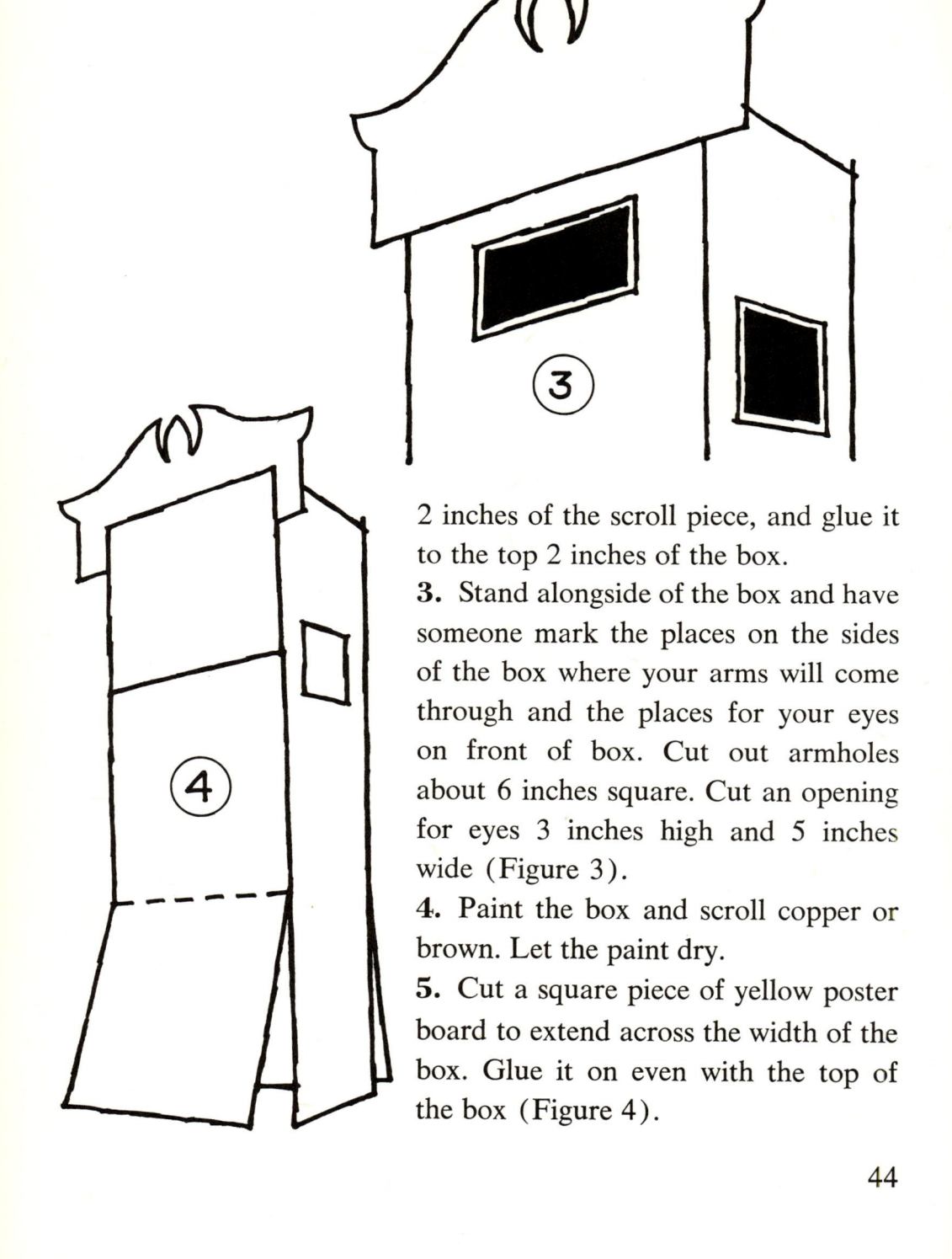

2 inches of the scroll piece, and glue it to the top 2 inches of the box.

3. Stand alongside of the box and have someone mark the places on the sides of the box where your arms will come through and the places for your eyes on front of box. Cut out armholes about 6 inches square. Cut an opening for eyes 3 inches high and 5 inches wide (Figure 3).

4. Paint the box and scroll copper or brown. Let the paint dry.

5. Cut a square piece of yellow poster board to extend across the width of the box. Glue it on even with the top of the box (Figure 4).

6. On the paper plate, print Roman numerals I through XII with marker or crayon. Glue the plate to the center of the yellow poster board. Draw two eyeholes the size of a pop-bottle cap and cut out through paper plate and yellow poster board. Draw a long and short clock hand on black paper. Cut out and glue the hands to the plate (Figure 5).

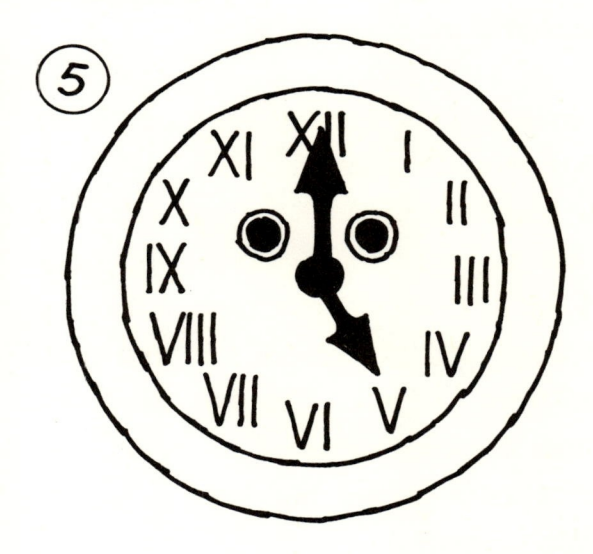

7. Cut a piece of white poster board 20 inches high and not quite as wide as the box. Draw and cut out a circle of yellow poster board as large as the rim of a drinking glass. From yellow poster board, cut out a strip 1 inch by

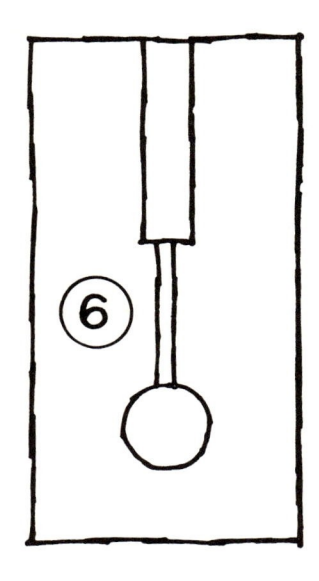

9 inches and another strip ½ inch by 6 inches. Glue an inch of one end of the small strip to the circle and an inch of the other end to the larger strip. This is the pendulum (Figure 6). Turn the pendulum over. Glue it on the white poster board, with the top placed at the top center of the white poster board.

8. Wear with a white or yellow long-sleeved shirt.

ANGEL

MATERIALS:

man's white shirt with long sleeves
   cut off just above the cuff slit
white material
   as long as the distance
   from your waist to the floor
   and as wide as twice
   your waist measurement
13 feet of 22-gauge wire
aluminum foil
blue tissue paper,
   about 2 feet square
household glue
cellophane tape
glitter

TOOLS:

scissors
tape measure
needle and
   white thread
newspapers
pliers or
   wire cutter
pencil

STEPS:

1. For the skirt, sew the two sides of the white material together, leaving a side opening 12 inches from the top (Figure 1).

2. With double thread, sew around the top of the skirt with basting stitches. Gather the skirt by pulling the thread until the skirt fits your waist. Tie the thread in a knot (Figure 2).

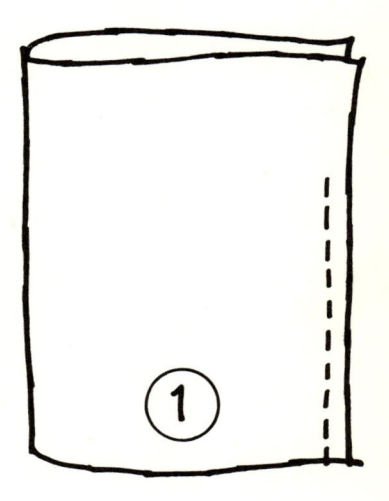

47

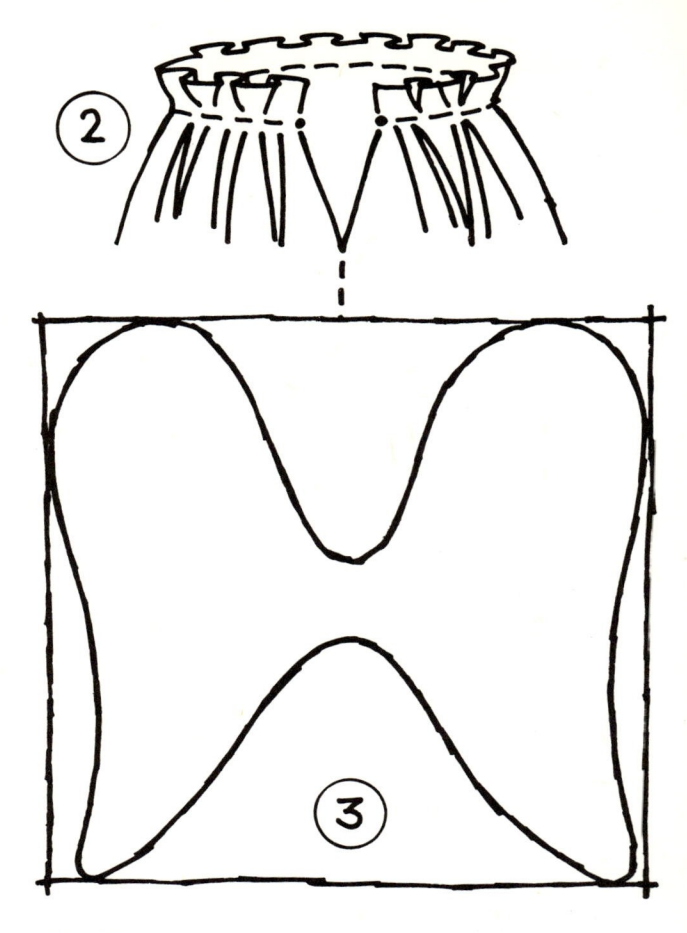

3. On a newspaper, draw and cut out the angel's wings. They should be about 20 inches wide and 20 inches high (Figure 3).

4. Lay the newspaper pattern on a flat surface. Starting at the center of the bottom, bend the wire to follow the outline of the pattern. Cut the wire and twist the ends together.

48

5. Cut ¾-inch strips of foil. Fold and crush the foil around the wire. Put glue along one side of the foil-covered wire. Lay the glued side on a sheet of blue tissue paper. Let the glue dry.

6. Cut out the tissue wings ¼ inch outside the wire.

7. Down the center of the back of the wings, overlap four strips of tape. Turn the wings over and put four more strips of tape in the same place (Figure 4). Measure the distance between the two top buttons on the shirt. Make two vertical slits, ½ inch long, this distance apart (Figure 5).

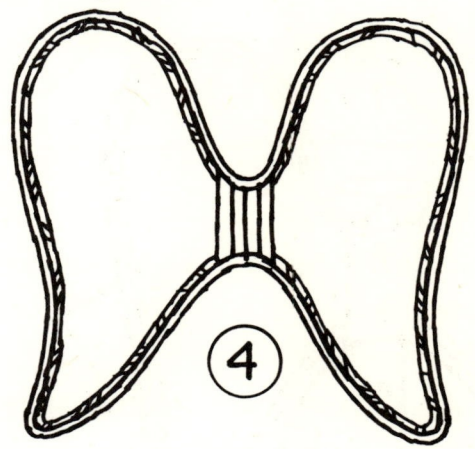

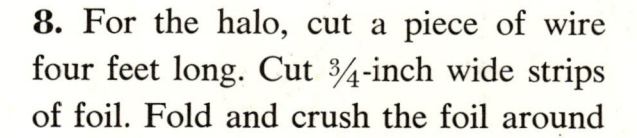

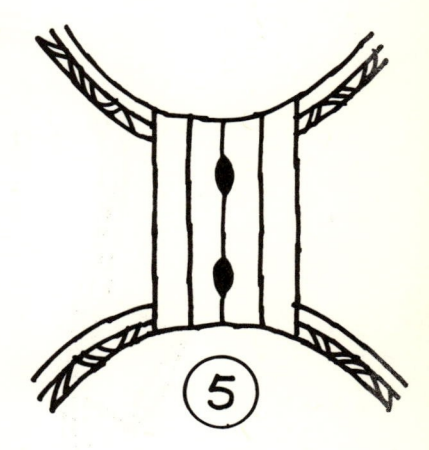

8. For the halo, cut a piece of wire four feet long. Cut ¾-inch wide strips of foil. Fold and crush the foil around the wire. Bend 18 inches of wire into a circle and twist together. Bend the halo circle halfway down. Bend the end of the wire into another circle big enough to fit your head. Twist the wire together. Bend this circle halfway up so it is parallel with the halo (Figure 6).

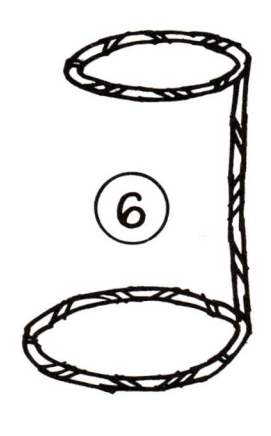

9. Apply glue on the swings and halo, and sprinkle with glitter.

10. Wear the shirt (turned backwards) over the skirt. Button the wings to the two top shirt buttons (Figure 7).

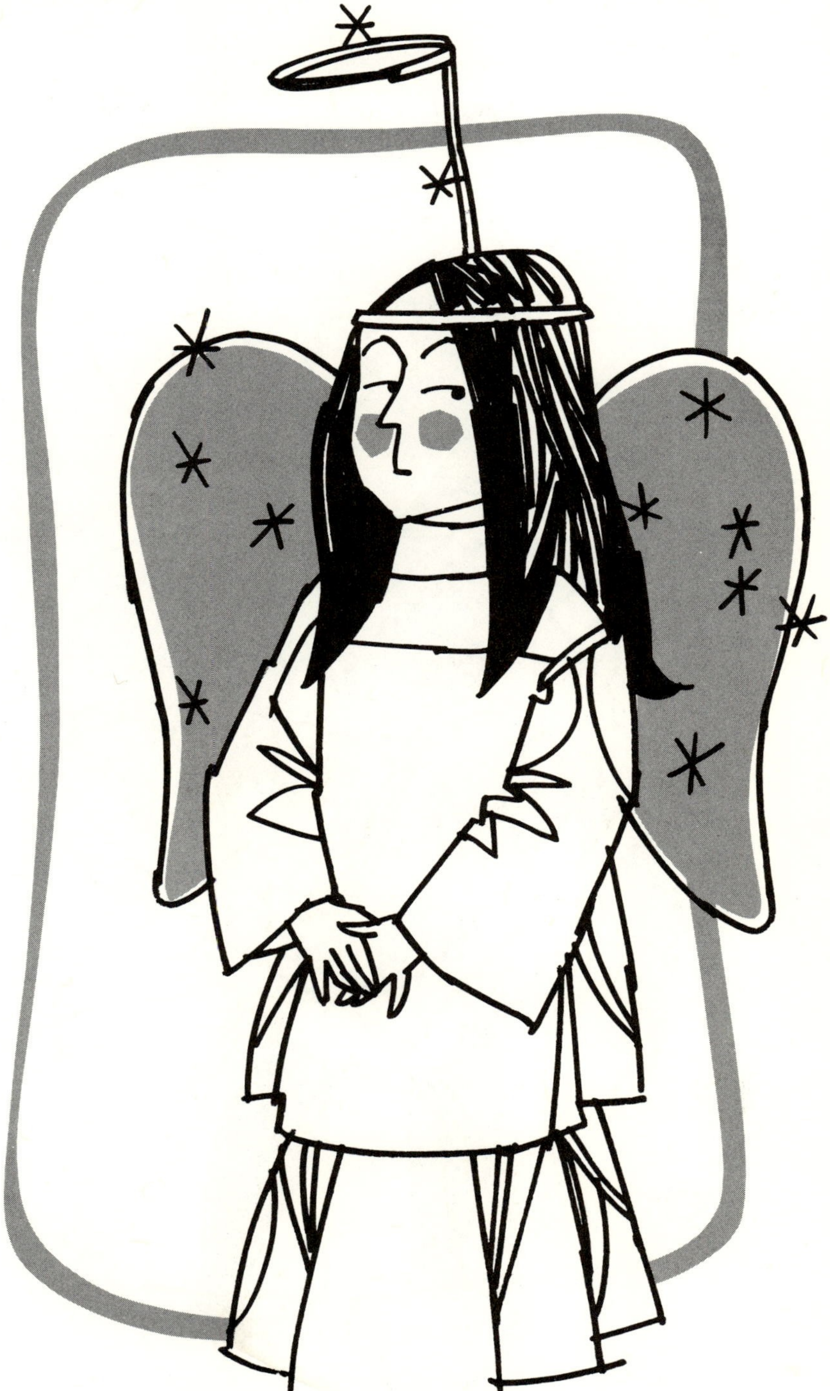

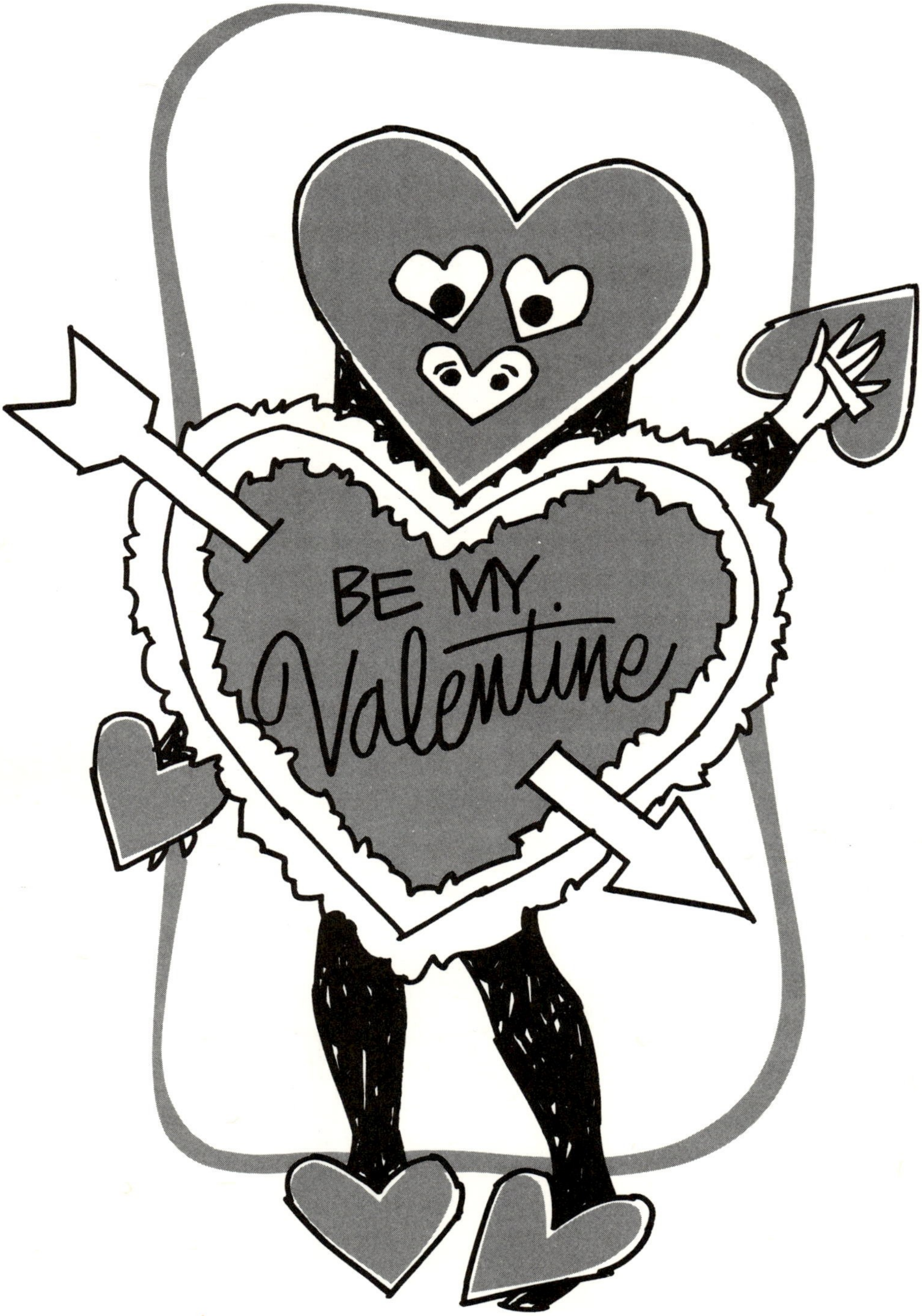
BE MY
Valentine

VALENTINE

MATERIALS:
white leotards or
   white pants and long-sleeved shirt
cardboard box large enough to fit
   comfortably over your body and
   to reach from your shoulders
   to just above your knees
cardboard box large enough to fit
   comfortably over your head
white paint
2 sheets red poster board,
   22 inches by 28 inches
½ yard white nylon net
household glue
glitter
white poster board
cellophane tape
thin cardboard

TOOLS:
scissors
pencil
paintbrush
newspapers
needle and
   white thread
stapler
white chalk
black crayon

STEPS:

1. Cut the lids and flaps off both boxes. The large box is the body of the costume; the small box is the head.

2. Cut a hole in the top of the large box big enough to fit over your head

53

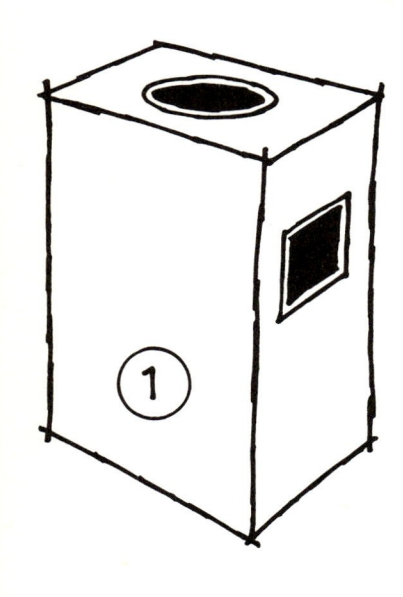

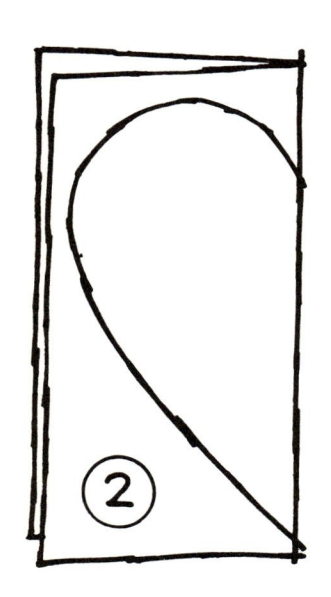

but smaller than the opening of the small box. Hold the box even with your shoulders and have someone mark places on the sides where your arms will come through. Cut out armholes 6 inches square (Figure 1).

3. Paint both boxes white. Let the paint dry.

4. Fold a piece of newspaper 22 inches by 28 inches in half, lengthwise. Draw half a heart on the fold (Figure 2). Unfold pattern, trace it on red poster board, and cut out. Make another smaller red heart the same way for the head box.

5. Cut strips of nylon net 2½ inches wide. Sew basting stitches along the center of a strip, pull the thread to gather the net, and tie the thread in a knot (Figure 3). Sew and gather enough strips to go all around the large heart.

6. Staple the center of the net ruffle along the edge of the heart.

7. Write a message such as *Be My Valentine* with white chalk on the large heart. Put glue along the chalk lines and sprinkle over with glitter.

8. On newspaper cut an arrow 20 inches long and 3 inches wide. Trace around this pattern on white poster board, and cut out. Cut the arrow in half. Cut a slit slightly wider than the arrow about 5 inches from edge of upper left part of heart and another slit 5 inches from edge of lower right part of heart. Insert the two pieces of the arrow 2 inches into the slits, and tape down on the back of the heart (Figure 4).

9. Hold the head box on one shoulder and have someone mark a line even with your eyes. At this level, cut an opening in center of the box, 6 inches across and 3 inches high. This is the mouth opening through which you will look.

10. Draw large heart-shaped eyes and a wide heart-shaped mouth on the smaller heart. Cut out the mouth. Paint the eyes white. After paint dries, draw a big black dot in the center.

11. Glue the smaller heart on the front of the head box, being certain that the mouth hole lines up with the hole in the box (Figure 5). Glue the larger heart on the front of the body box.

12. From red poster board, cut out four small hearts the size of your hand. Across the center back of two hearts, tape an inch-wide strip of thin cardboard in a loop allowing enough space for your hands to slip through just below the thumbs. Do the same with the other two hearts leaving enough space to slip them over your feet (Figure 6).

13. Glue or tape the small box on the center top of the large box.

14. Wear the small hearts on your hands and feet. Have someone help you into the boxes.

BUTTERFLY

MATERIALS:
black leotards or
    black pants and long-sleeved shirt
9-gauge aluminum wire
    as long as 4 times the distance
    from your shoulders to floor
lace curtain or very thin material
black plastic tape
black belt or
    strip of black material,
    3 inches by 36 inches
strip of black material,
    2 inches by 25 inches
2 black chenille stems or
    4 pipe cleaners, painted black

TOOLS:
newspapers
ruler
scissors
crayon
needle and thread
clip clothespins
black thread

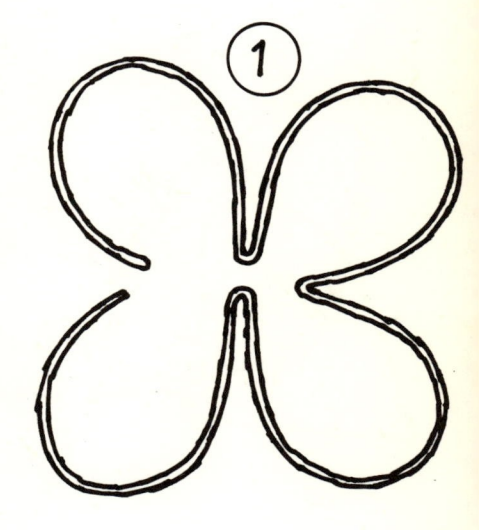

STEPS:

1. With tape, mark the wire into four equal parts. Bend each of the four parts into a circle (Figure 1).

2. Twist the two ends of the wire bringing the four circles together (Figure 2).

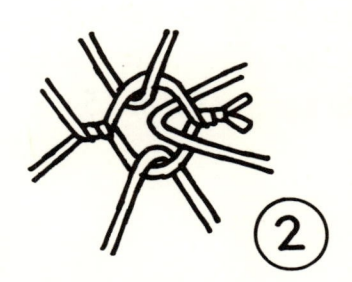

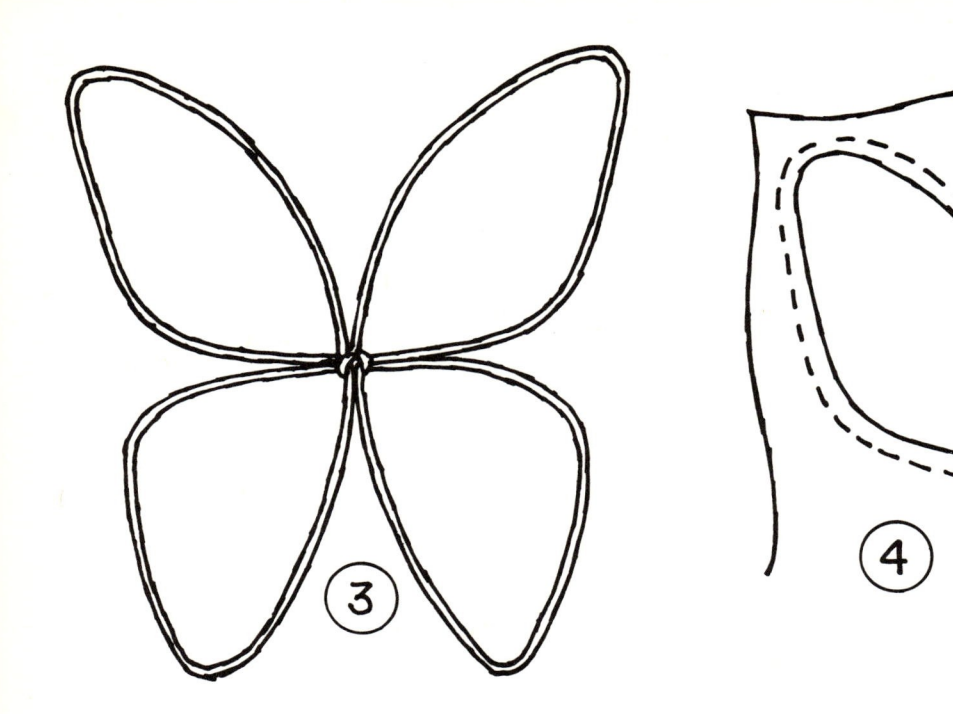

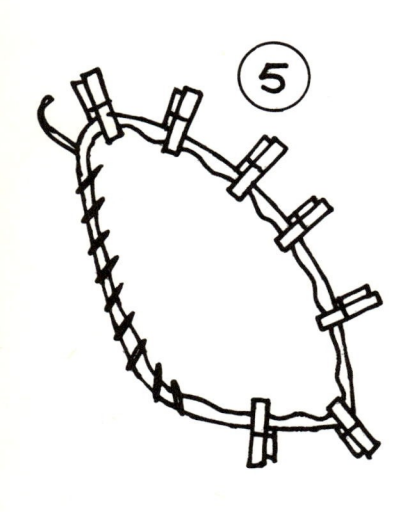

3. Bend each circle into the shape of a butterfly wing (Figure 3).

4. Lay a newspaper under each wing, and, with a crayon, draw around the wire to make a pattern. Cut out patterns. Lay each pattern on the curtain or material, and cut out an inch larger all the way around (Figure 4).

5. Clip the four pieces of material to the wire with clothespins, folding the edges an inch over the wire.

6. Sew the material to the wire with an overcast stitch (Figure 5).

58

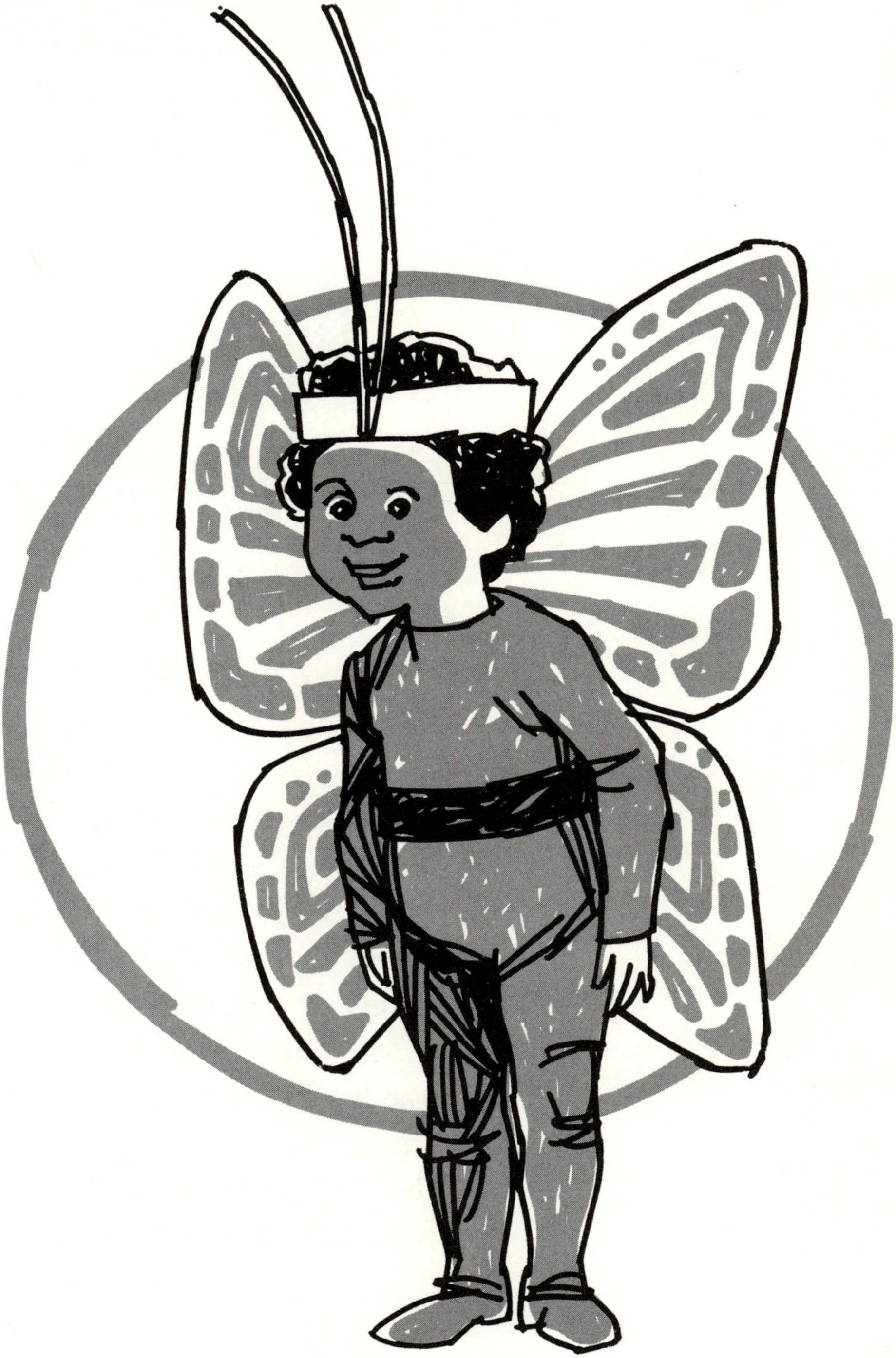

7. Decorate the wings with a pattern of spots and lines cut out of black tape.
8. Tape the center back of belt or strip of black material to the front center of the butterfly (Figure 6).

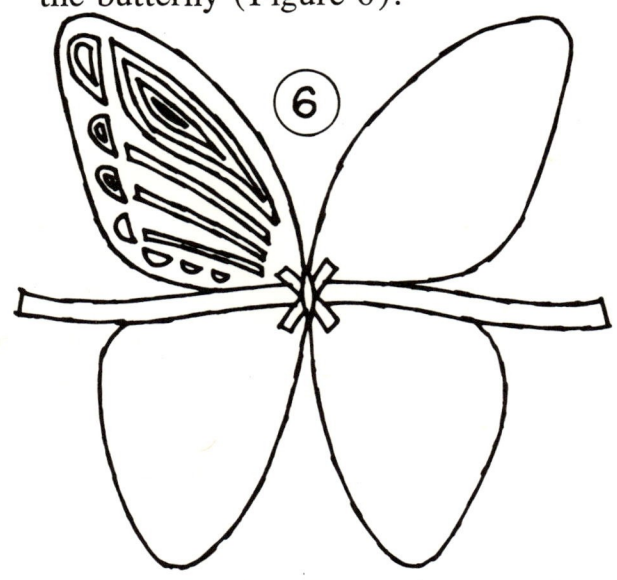

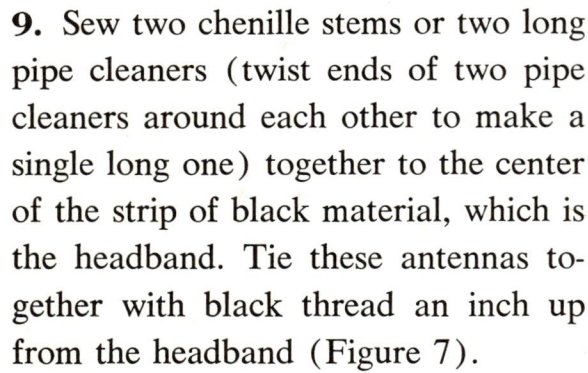

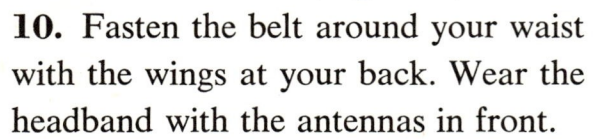

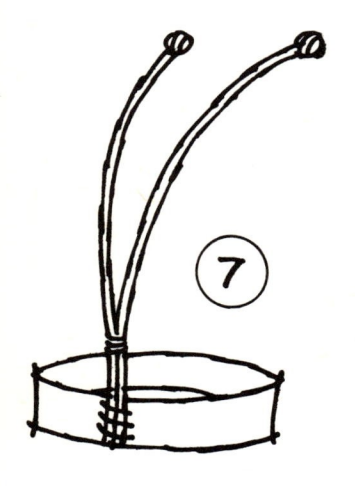

9. Sew two chenille stems or two long pipe cleaners (twist ends of two pipe cleaners around each other to make a single long one) together to the center of the strip of black material, which is the headband. Tie these antennas together with black thread an inch up from the headband (Figure 7).
10. Fasten the belt around your waist with the wings at your back. Wear the headband with the antennas in front.

FROG

MATERIALS:

green leotards or
   green long-sleeved shirt and pants
large balloon
paper towels
flour and water
pressed-cardboard egg carton
household glue
green poster paint
white poster paint
green construction paper
thin cardboard

TOOLS:

scissors
ruler
pencil
paintbrush
newspaper
black felt-tip
   marker or crayon

STEPS:

1. Blow up the balloon to a size bigger than your head.
2. Tear paper towels into strips.
3. Mix flour and water in a large bowl to make a liquid paste. Dip one strip of paper towel at a time into the paste and stick it to the balloon. Cover the whole balloon, applying the strips in different directions (Figure 1). Paste two more layers of strips over the balloon. Let dry for at least a day.
4. When thoroughly dry, cut off the

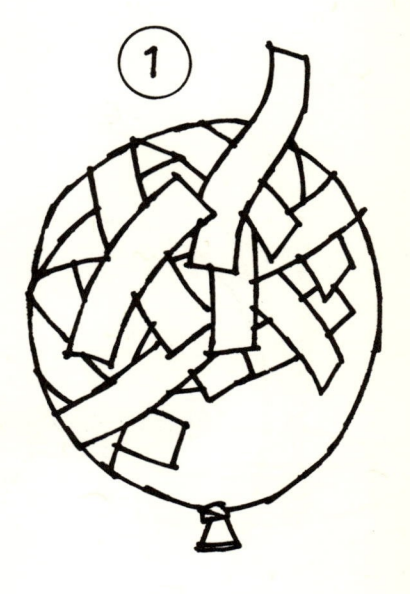

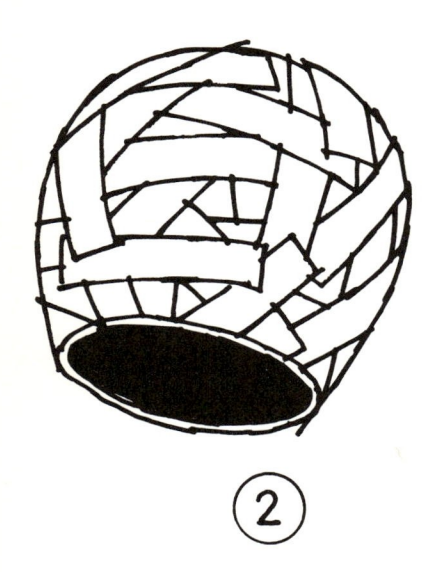

bottom so opening will fit over your head (Figure 2). Remove balloon.

5. Put the head on and have someone mark the places for your eyes. Remove the head and at the eye marks, draw a long straight mouth, an inch wide, going across the whole front of the head. Cut out the mouth, through which you will look (Figure 3).

6. Dip strips of paper towel in the paste and build up several layers around the mouth.

7. For eyes, cut two egg cups from carton. Glue on eyes about 4½ inches above the mouth and 5½ inches apart. With strips of towel dipped in the paste, build up a layer around the eyes (Figure 4). Let dry.

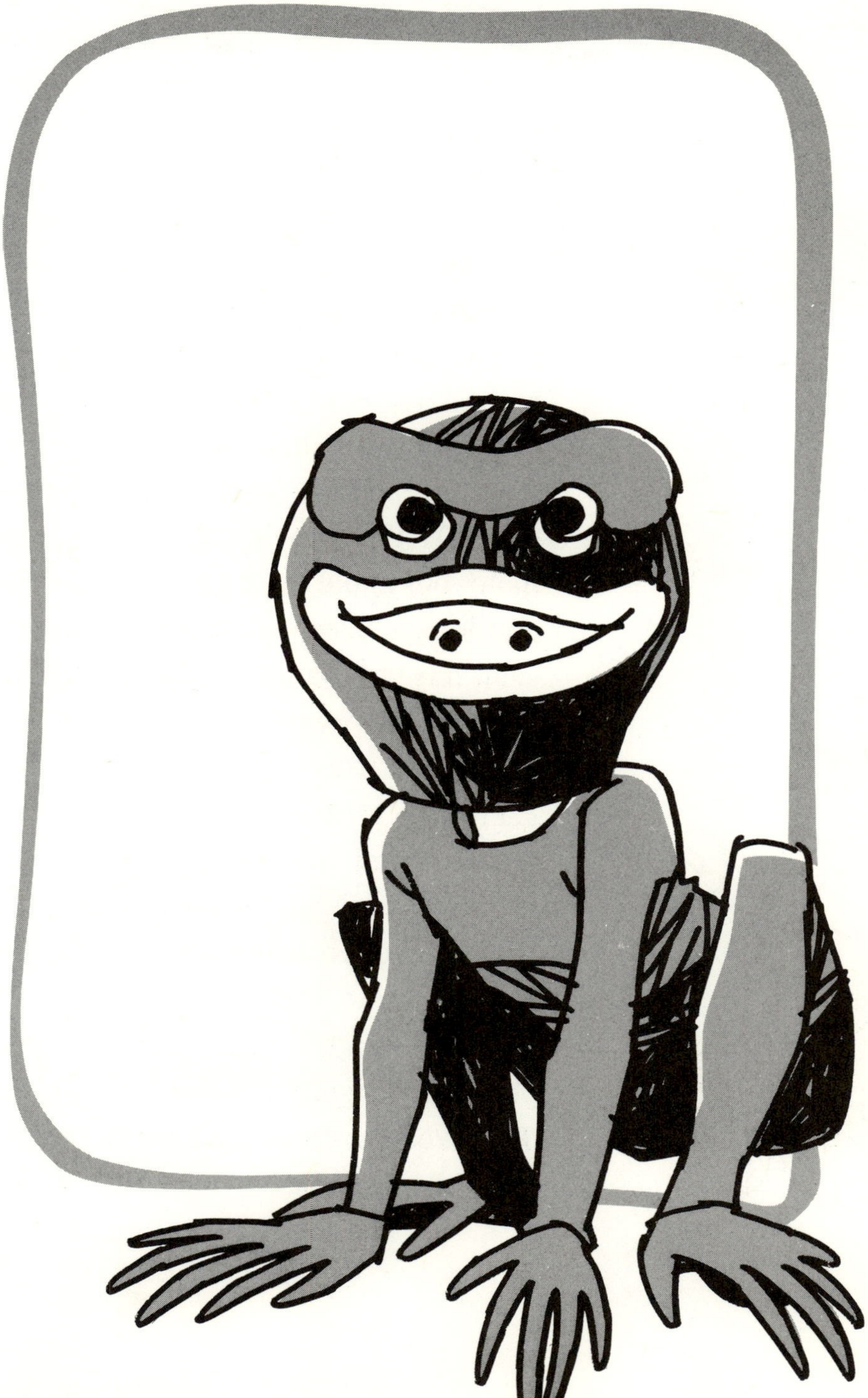

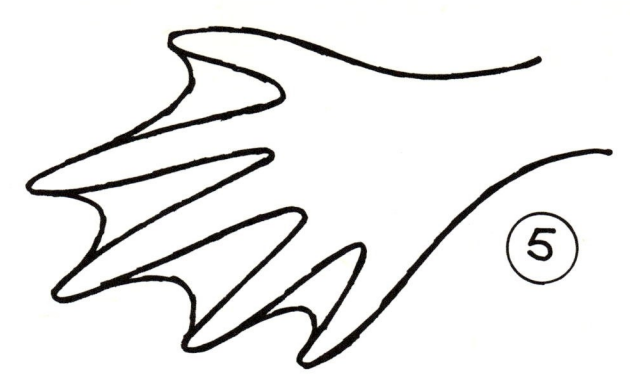

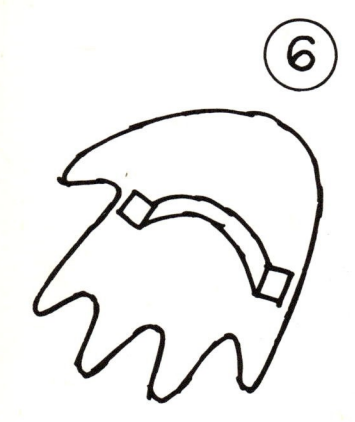

8. Paint the frog's head green and the mouth and eyes white. When the paint is dry, draw a black center in the eyes with marker or crayon.

9. Place your hand, palm down, on newspaper with your fingers spread apart. With a pencil, trace around your hand, but make the fingers a little wider and longer. Draw a web mark between each finger (Figure 5). Using this as a pattern, cut out four frog's feet from green construction paper. Across the center back of two feet, glue an inch-wide strip of thin cardboard in a loop allowing enough space for your hands to slip through just below the thumbs. Do the same with the other two feet leaving enough space to slip them over your feet (Figure 6). Let the glue dry.

10. Wear costume with green leotards or shirt and pants.

BUNNY

MATERIALS:

3 white towels of equal size
   (bath towels if you are
   over 3 feet 6 inches;
   hand towels if you are
   under 3 feet 6 inches)
2 pairs of men's white socks
wad of cotton
scrap of white cloth
   or white tissue
2 white paper bags,
   one with a flat bottom and
   large enough to fit comfortably
   over your head, the other
   at least 9 inches long
rubber bands
household glue
cellophane tape

TOOLS:

pencil
needle and
   white thread
straight pins
ruler
scissors
black crayon
pink crayon
safety pins

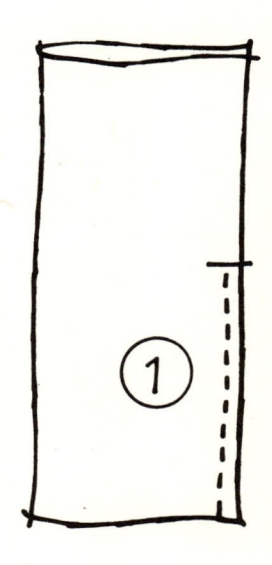

STEPS:

Body:

1. Fold two towels lengthwise and mark the center of the open edge of each towel with a pencil. Sew the sides of each towel together to the center point (Figure 1).

65

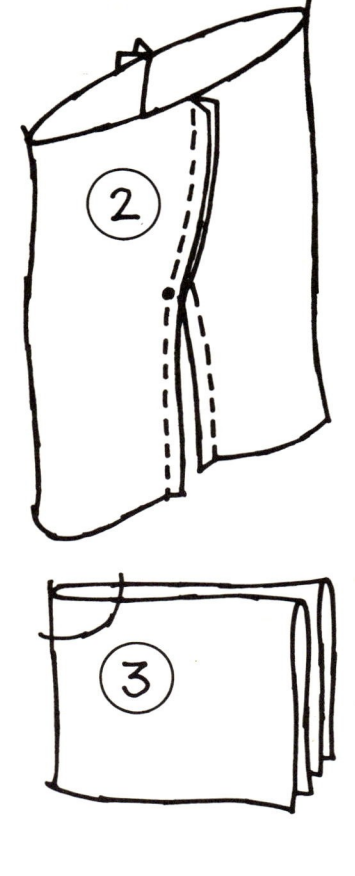

2. Lay the towels side by side with the seams placed alongside each other. Pin the front of the two towels together, starting at the top of the leg seams. Sew together. Repeat the same step for the back (Figure 2).

3. Fold the third towel lengthwise, then crosswise. At the folded corner measure 2½ inches down each side. Draw a curved line between marks and cut off (Figure 3).

4. With the towel folded lengthwise, lay above the leg section. Be sure the centers of both sections meet.

5. Pin the front of the top section to the front of the leg section, and sew them together. Do the same for the back top and leg sections. Sew together the two bottom edges of each sleeve (Figure 4).

6. From the center neck edge, cut a slit part way down the back. Turn costume inside out.

7. Make a tail by gluing a wad of cotton to a scrap of cloth or white tissue. Pin to costume (Figure 5).

8. Have someone pin the costume together at the back opening.

9. Wear white socks. Bind the pant legs at the ankles with a rubber band. Wear the other pair of socks over your hands. Bind the sleeves to your forearms with rubber bands.

Head:

1. Fold up the top of the flat-bottomed bag about 2 inches. Put the bag over your head.

2. With a crayon, mark the places for your eyes and mouth. Take the bag off. With a pencil, draw eyes, nose, and mouth (Figure 6).

3. Cut out the eyes and mouth. With black crayon, outline the eye holes.

Ears:

1. On the other white bag, at the side

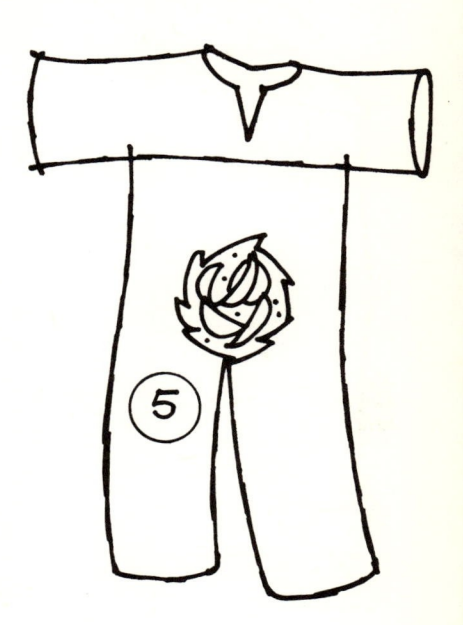

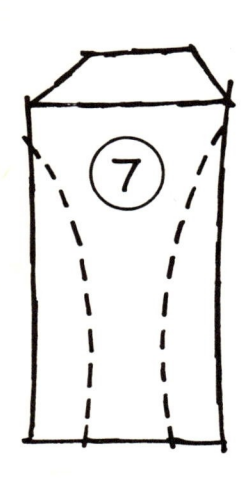

creases, draw ears 3½ inches wide and 9 inches high (Figure 7). Cut out.

2. Color the inside of the ears and outline the nose and mouth with pink crayon.

3. Tape the bottom of the ears 1½ inches below the top of the back corners of the head. Be sure the creases of the ears are even with the creases of the bag (Figure 8).

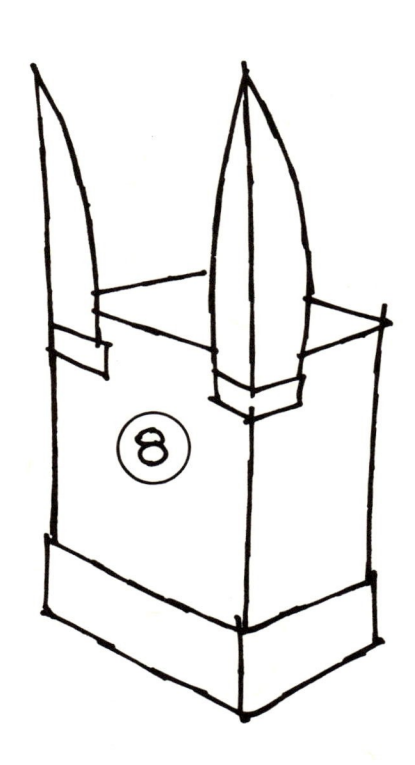

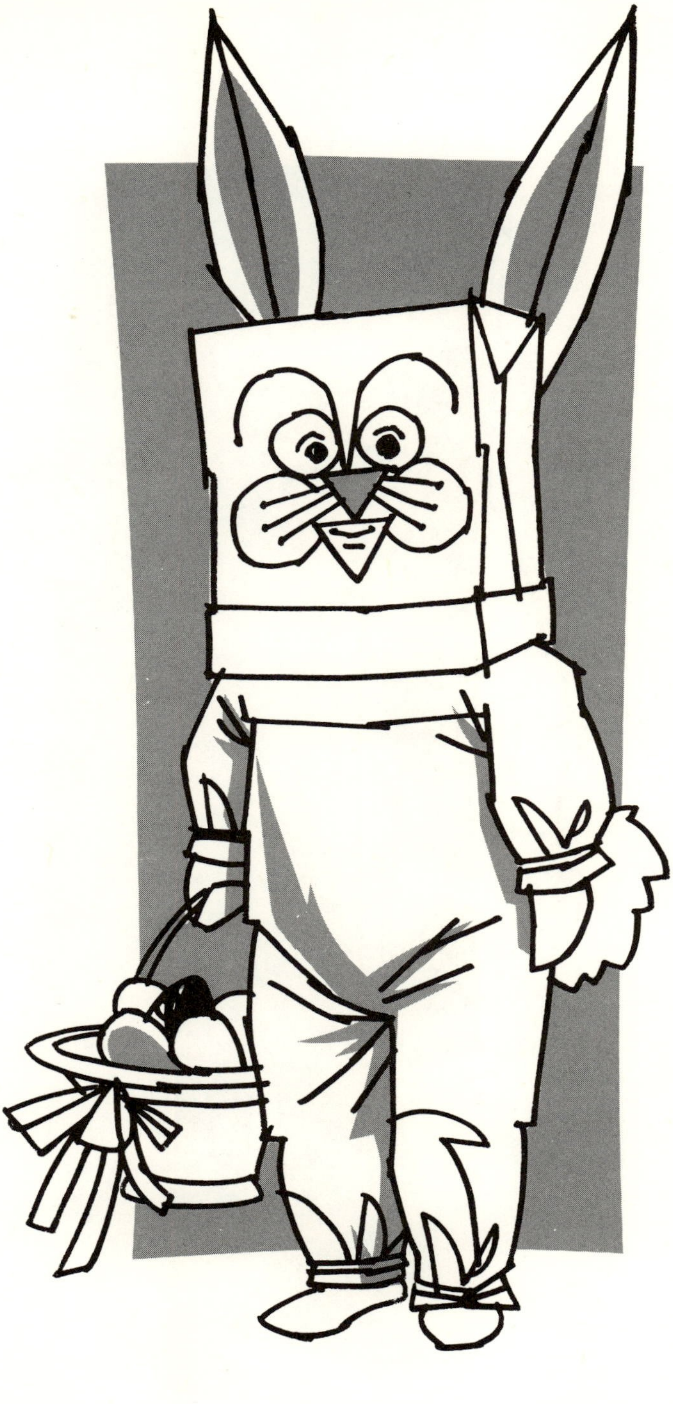

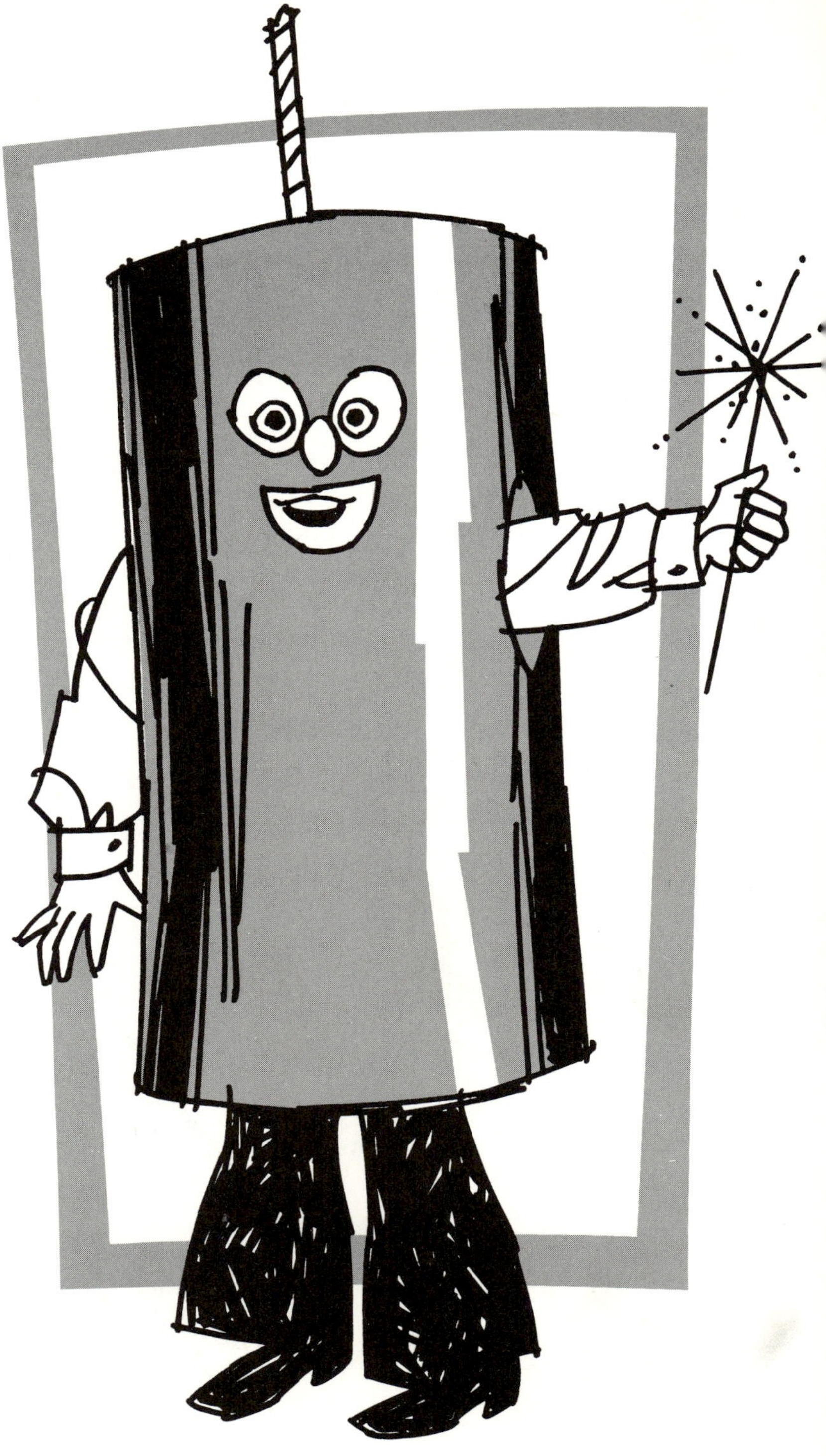

FIRECRACKER

MATERIALS:
long-sleeved white shirt and
 dark pants
5 sheets of poster board,
 each 22 inches by 28 inches
masking tape
household glue
red paint
white paint
1 foot of heavy rope
 about ¾ inch in diameter

TOOLS:
stapler
pencil
ruler
scissors
clip clothespins
paintbrush

STEPS:

1. Lay two sheets of poster board on the floor with the long sides overlapping ½ inch. Tape the overlapped sides together on both sides. Do the same thing with two more sheets of poster board. Lay the sheets on the floor next to each other. Overlap a sheet ½ inch over the other sheet and tape both together. Turn over and tape the overlapped seam on the back (Figure 1).

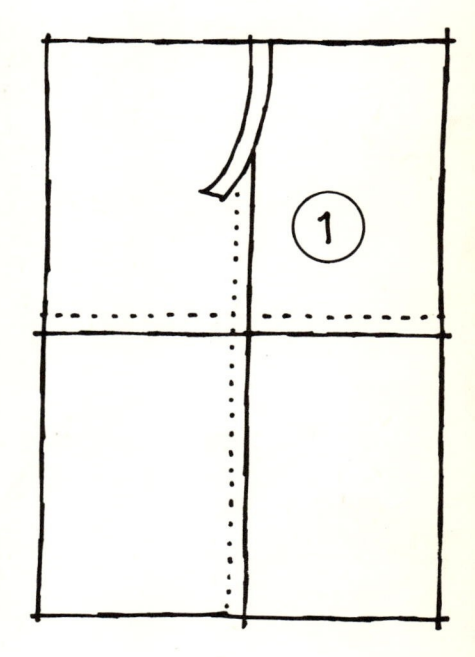

2. Stand the poster board up. Have someone curve it into a cylinder around you, overlapping the ends so you have enough room to be comfortable. Have the person staple the cylinder together at the top and bottom (Figure 2). Take the cylinder off. Tape the cylinder together all the way down the outside and the inside.

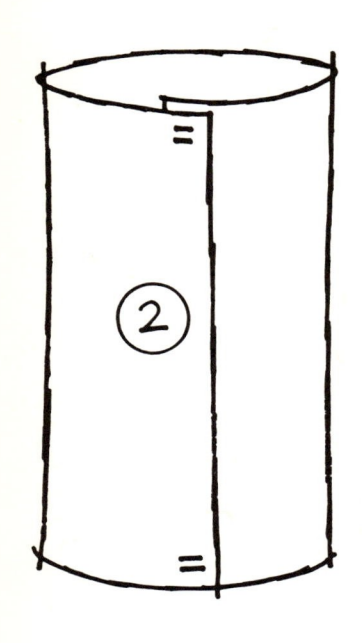

3. Set the cylinder on another sheet of poster board. Trace around it with a pencil. Draw another circle about 2 inches outside the first circle. Cut out the large circle. Cut slits to the inside circle an inch apart. The slits make the tabs. Bend the tabs up (Figure 3).

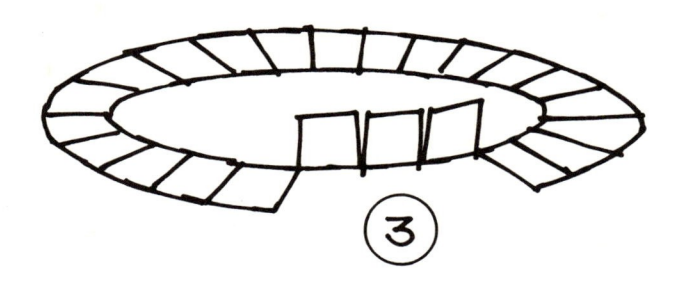

4. Put a line of glue 2 inches wide around the inside top of the firecracker. Set the cardboard circle on the top of the firecracker, and gently push the center down until the tops of the tabs are even with the top of the firecracker

72

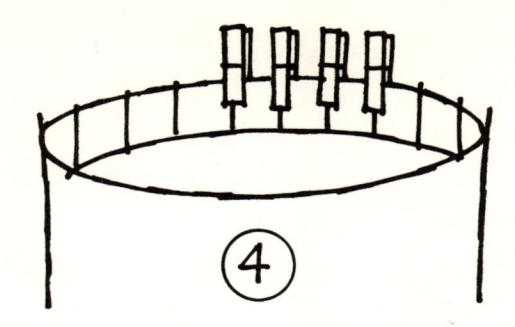

(Figure 4). Clip clothespins to the tabs until the glue dries.

5. Put cylinder over your body and have someone mark places for your eyes, mouth, and arms. Remove cylinder and draw and cut out eyeholes and mouth opening. Cut out large armholes (Figure 5).

6. Paint the firecracker red. Let the paint dry.

7. With pencil, draw large circles around the eyeholes, and draw a nose. Paint with white paint.

8 The rope is the firecracker fuse. Apply glue all over it. Let the glue dry. Glue one end to the top of the firecracker. Prop it up until the glue dries. Then apply glue all around the bottom edge of the fuse.

9. Have someone help you get into the costume.

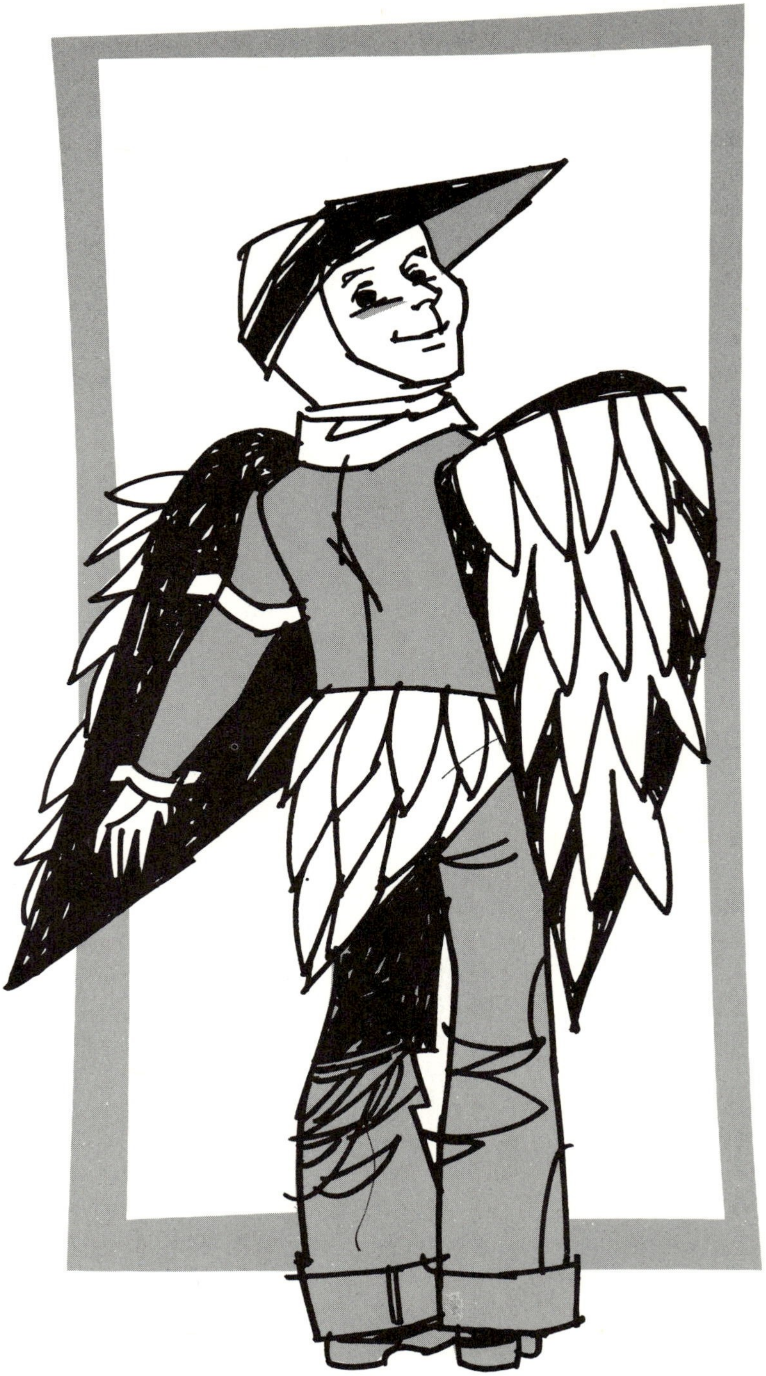

REDHEADED WOODPECKER

MATERIALS:

dark leotards or
   dark pants and long-sleeved shirt
piece of red material,
   26 inches by 19 inches
3 sheets black poster board,
   22 inches by 28 inches
crepe or tissue paper,
   yellow, black, and white
household glue
black cord or shoelaces
paper clip

TOOLS:

newspaper
pencil
ruler
scissors
straight pins
tape measure
needle and
   red thread
stapler

STEPS:

Hood:

1. Fold a newspaper, and draw a pattern for the front of a hood. Fold an-

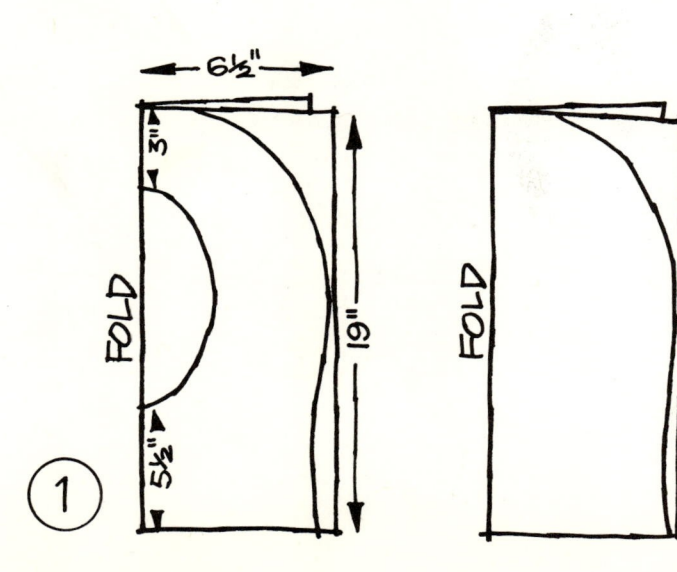

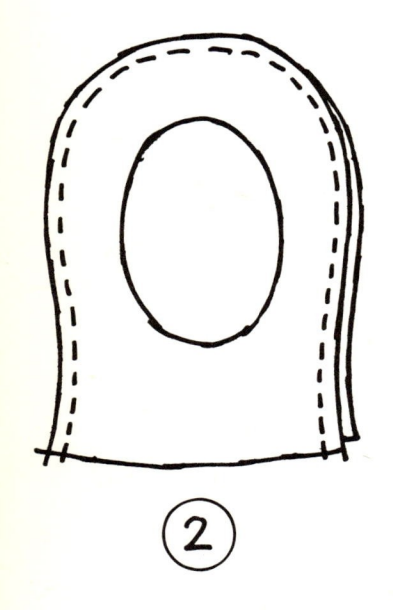

other newspaper, and draw a pattern for the back of a hood (Figure 1). Cut out both patterns.

2. Cut the red material into two pieces, each 13 inches by 19 inches. Put the unfolded pattern for the front of the hood on one piece of material and the pattern for the back of the hood on the other. Pin on the patterns and cut out.

3. Lay the front of the hood on the back of the hood, right sides together, and pin. Sew ½ inch from the outside edges all the way up one side, across the top, and down the other side. Leave the bottom open (Figure 2). Turn right side out.

Wings:

1. Measure your arm from the top of your shoulder to the tips of your fingers. Draw a line this length on a newspaper (A). This is the length of each wing. Draw a line half this long perpendicular to center of the first line (B). This is the width of the wing. Using these lines as a guide, draw the wing pattern (Figure 3). Cut out.

2. Lay the pattern on black poster

76

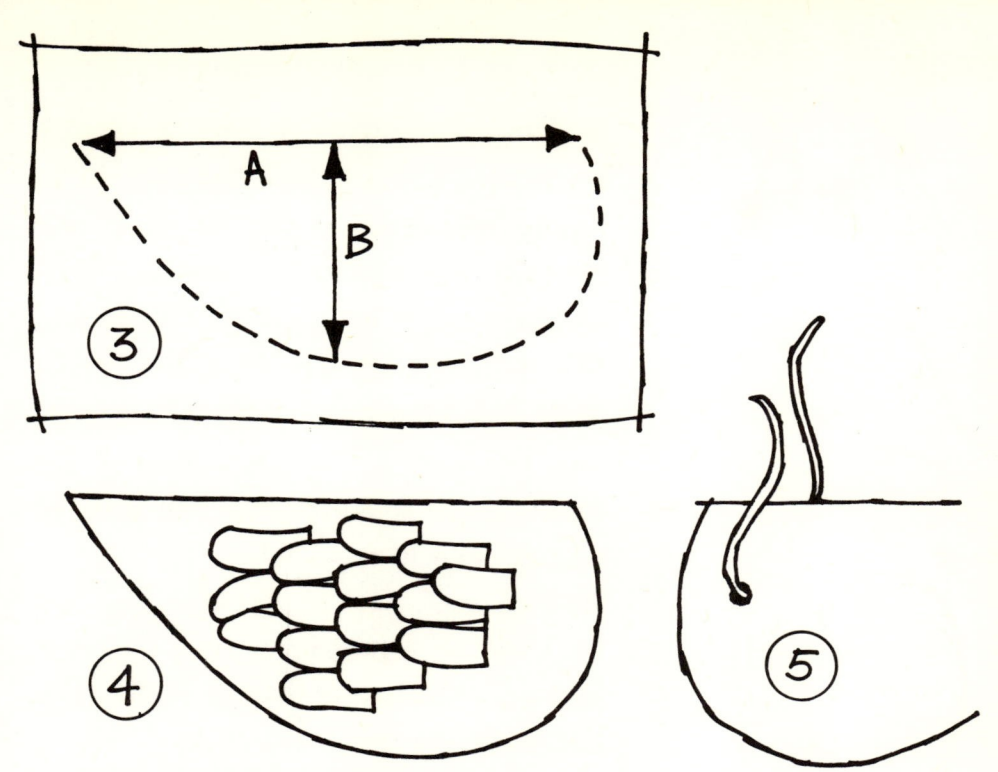

board. Trace around it, and cut out. Make another wing the same way.

3. From the crepe or tissue paper, cut out pieces 2½ by 5 inches for feathers. You can cut several at a time by folding the paper. Round out the corners at one end. Glue the straight ends of the feathers to the wings (Figure 4).

4. At the center shoulder end of each wing, make a small hole an inch from the edge. Draw a cord or shoelace through each hole (Figure 5). Tie the wings at your shoulders when you wear the costume.

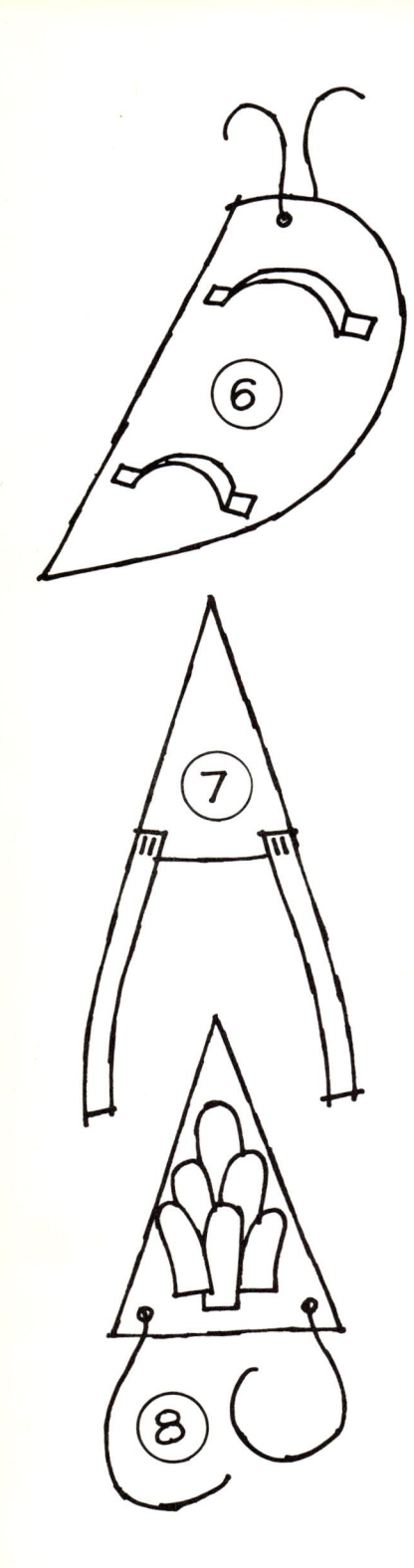

5. Cut two strips of black poster board an inch wide and 10 inches long. Staple crosswise to the backs of the wings 6 inches from the shoulder ends. Cut two more strips an inch wide and 8 inches long. Staple crosswise to the back of the wings 6 inches from the tips. In stapling the strips, make loops to allow enough space for your arms to slip through (Figure 6).

Beak:

1. Draw a triangle on black poster board, 10 inches high and 7 inches at the base. Cut out. At each angle of the base, staple a strip of black cardboard, 1½ inches by 12 inches (Figure 7). Wear around your head over the hood, with the strip fastened at the back with a paper clip.

Tail:

1. Draw a triangle on black poster board, 13 inches high and 10 inches at the base. Cut out. Cover with paper feathers as you did the wings.

2. One inch from each angle of the base, make a small hole. Tie a cord through each hole, and tie the cords around your waist (Figure 8).

POODLE

MATERIALS:

white leotards or
  white pants and long-sleeved sweater
white material,
  26 inches by 19 inches
white nylon net, 3 yards
4 white chenille stems,
  each 10 inches long,
  or 8 white pipe cleaners
  (twist ends of two pipe cleaners
  together to make a single long one)
white plastic foam cup
strip of cardboard,
  1¼ inches by 15 inches
pink or red paint
jingle bell
aluminum foil
household glue

TOOLS:

newspapers
pencil
ruler
scissors
straight pins
safety pin
needle and
  white thread
white elastic thread
black felt-tip
  marker or crayon
paintbrush
paper clip

STEPS:

Hood:

1. Fold a newspaper, and draw a pattern for the front of the hood. Fold another newspaper, and draw a pattern for the back of the hood (Figure 1). Cut out both patterns.

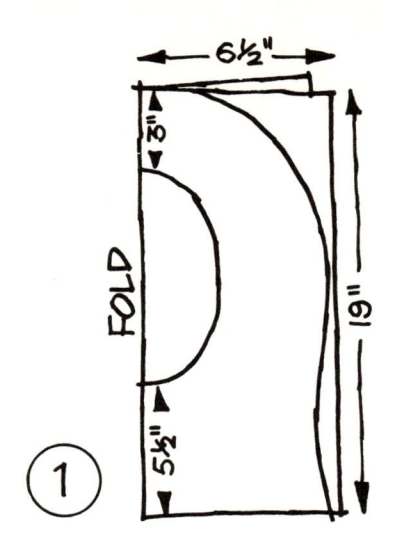

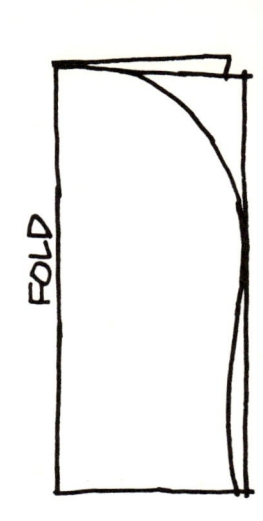

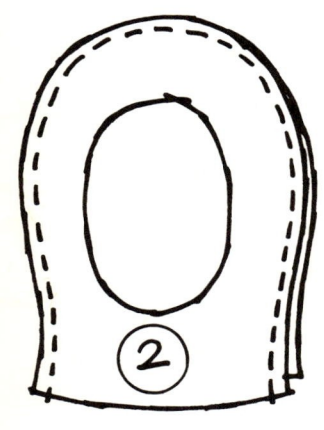

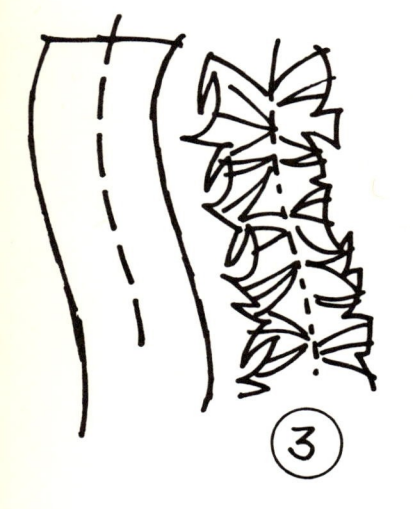

2. Cut the material into two pieces, each 13 inches by 19 inches. Pin one unfolded pattern on each piece of material and cut out.

3. Lay the front of the hood on the back of the hood, right sides together, and pin. Sew ½ inch from the edge all the way up one side, across the top, and down the other side. Leave the bottom open. Turn right side out (Figure 2).

Pompons:

1. Cut a 6-inch-wide strip from nylon net, crosswise. Using a double thread, sew down the center with basting stitches. Pull thread to gather the strip until it is 7 inches long (Figure 3).

80

2. Wrap the end of the thread twice around the center of the gathered strip, and tie it into a round pompon (Figure 4). Make seven more pompons the same way.

3. Sew three pompons across the top of the hood at the seam. Sew two pompons together loosely at the outer edges to make an ear. Sew two more pompons together to make another ear. Sew each ear to the edge of each outer pompon on the hood (Figure 5).

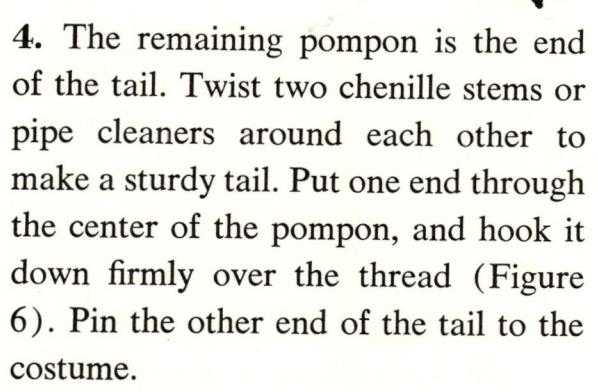

4. The remaining pompon is the end of the tail. Twist two chenille stems or pipe cleaners around each other to make a sturdy tail. Put one end through the center of the pompon, and hook it down firmly over the thread (Figure 6). Pin the other end of the tail to the costume.

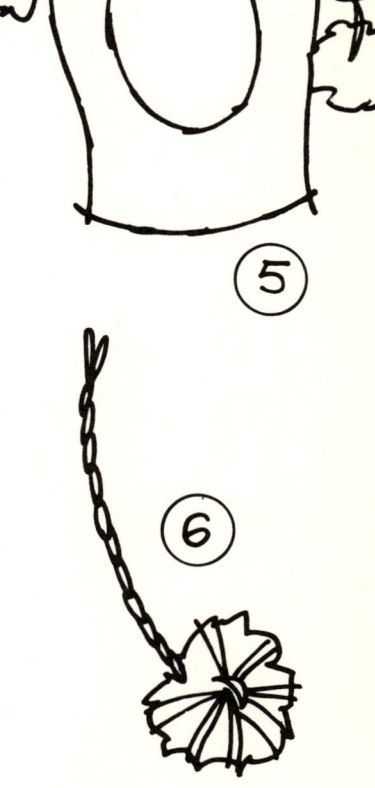

5. For the leg and wrist pompons, cut four double strips of nylon net 6 inches wide, crosswise (Figure 7). Using elastic thread, sew basting stitches down the middle of each double strip. Pull the threads to gather the net so the pompons fit loosely around your ankles and wrists, and tie.

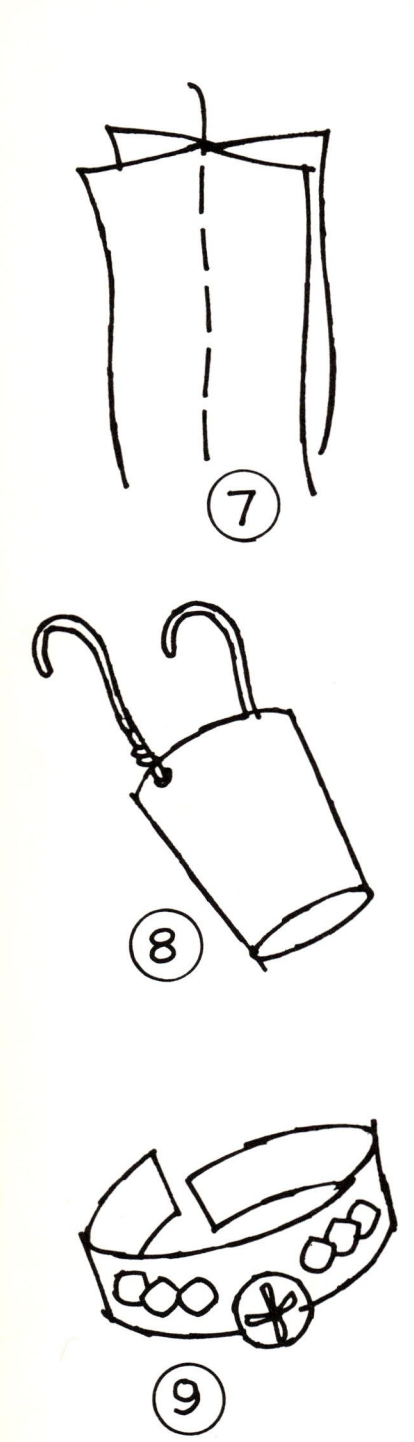

Nose:

1. On opposite sides of the plastic foam cup, make small holes ½ inch from the top. Put an inch of one end of a chenille stem or pipe cleaner through one hole and twist firmly around the stem base. Do the same at the other hole (Figure 8). Bend the ends around your ears to hold the nose in place.

2. With black marker or crayon, make markings on the end of the nose.

Collar:

1. Paint one side of the cardboard pink or red. Let the paint dry. In the center front of the cardboard, sew on the bell.

2. Roll six pieces of foil into little balls about the size of your fingertip. Glue three on each side of the bell for jewels (Figure 9). Fasten the collar around your neck with a paper clip.

3. Wear all the parts with white leotards or white pants and sweater.

82

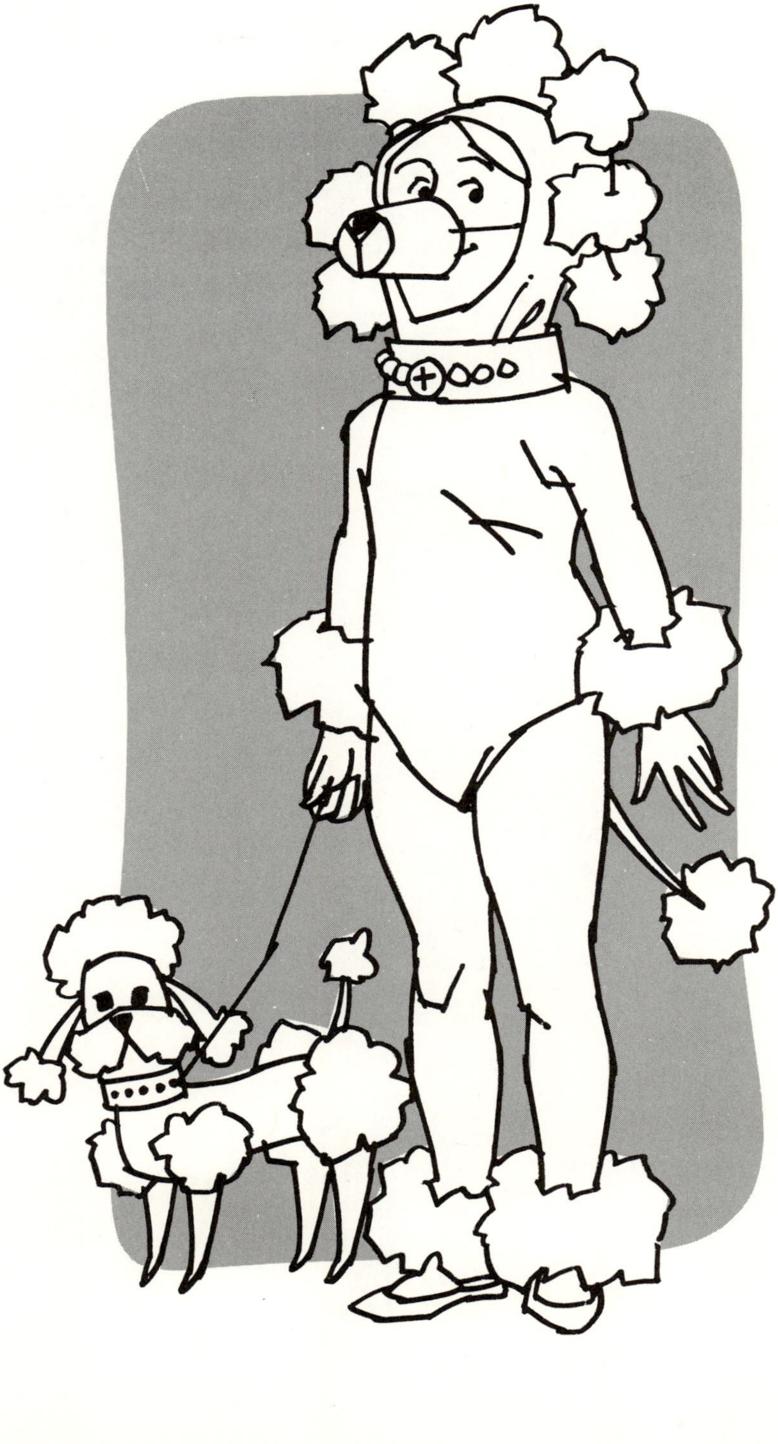

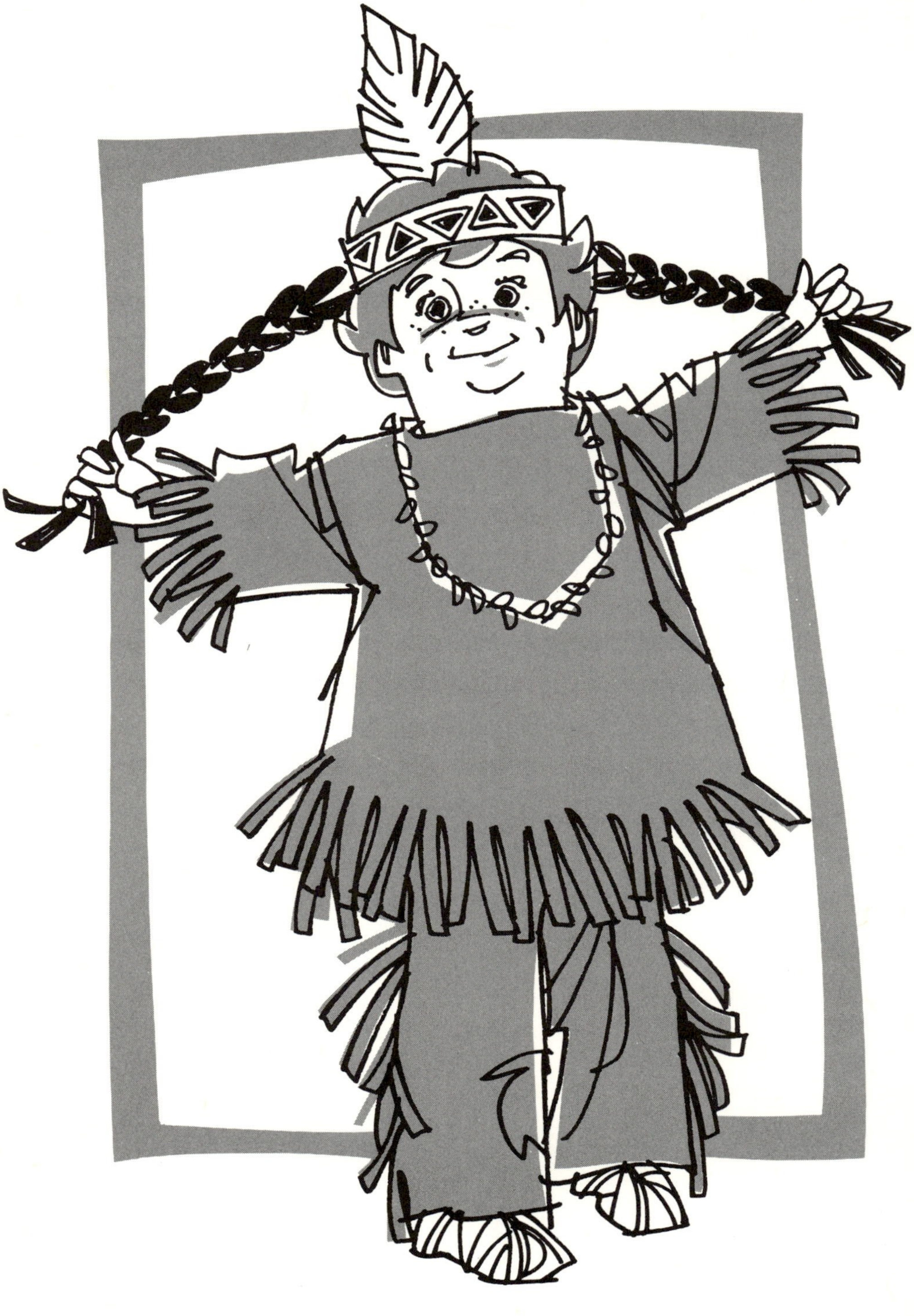

INDIAN

MATERIALS:

double-sized sheet dyed brown, or
  brown material
elastic for waistband
strip of thin cardboard or
  construction paper,
  1¼ inches by 25 inches
red construction paper
household glue
black material,
  9 inches by 26 inches
green and blue food coloring
masking tape
2 pieces of aluminum foil
  about 12 inches by 15 inches
black or brown enamel paint
dried lima beans (about 125)
heavy sewing thread

TOOLS:

tape measure
ruler
light chalk
scissors
straight pins
needle and thread
safety pin
felt-tip marker
  or crayon
paper clip or
  stapler
paintbrush

STEPS:

Dress for Girls or Shirt for Boys:

1. Have someone measure the distance from your shoulders to your knees for the length of dress. You will need twice this length of material. Length of shirt is 8 inches less. With your arms held straight out at the sides, have distance measured from elbow to elbow for the width of dress.

2. Fold the brown sheet or material crosswise, wrong side out. With chalk, mark lines for length (A) and width (B). Measure down each side 8½ inches from the top, and draw a line 6 inches toward the center; these are the sleeves. From the underarms, draw lines straight down (C); these are the sides of the dress or shirt (Figure 1). Cut on the lines.

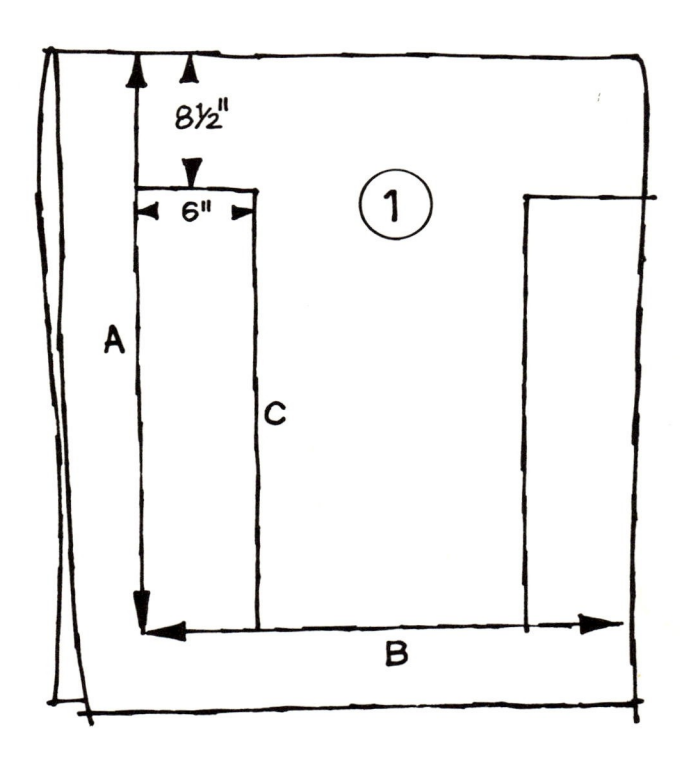

3. Pin the two pieces together, and sew a seam ½ inch from the edge on both sides and extending to end of sleeves. Turn right side out.

4. Fold the garment lengthwise in the center. At the top folded corner, measure 2½ inches down each side. Draw a curved line between marks and cut out (Figure 2). Unfold and cut a slit down the center front large enough for your head to go through opening.

5. For fringe, cut 3-inch slits every ¾ inch around the bottom of the dress or shirt and the ends of the sleeves (Figure 3).

Pants:

1. Have someone measure the distance from your waist to the floor; add an inch. You will need twice this length of material. Measure around your waist; add 12 inches. This is the width.

2. Fold the material crosswise, right side out. Draw lines for length (A) and width (B). Cut on the lines. Pin the two pieces together. Draw a line (C) halfway up the center (Figure 4).

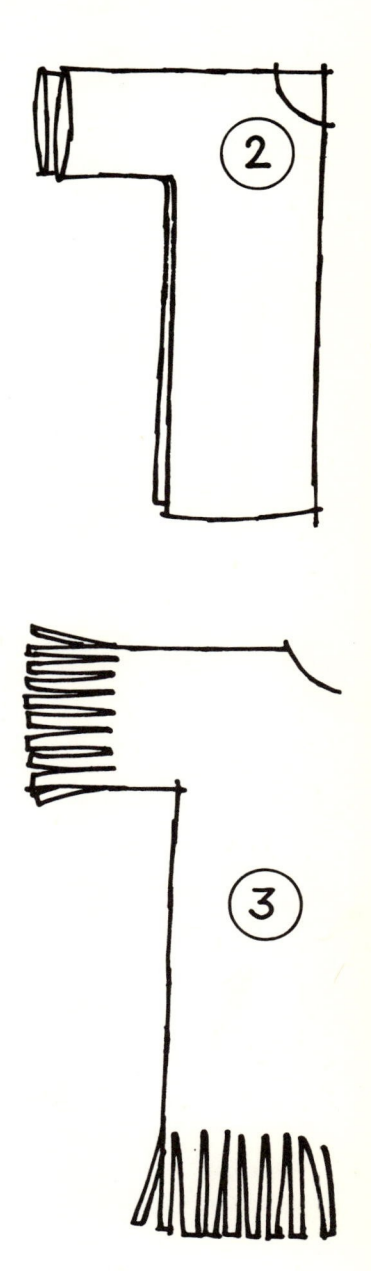

3. Sew a seam ½ inch outside line C on each side. Cut on the line, being careful not to snip the stitches. Starting 1½ inches down from the fold, sew the sides together 2 inches from the edges. For fringe, cut 1½-inch slits every ¾ inch along both sides (Figure 5).

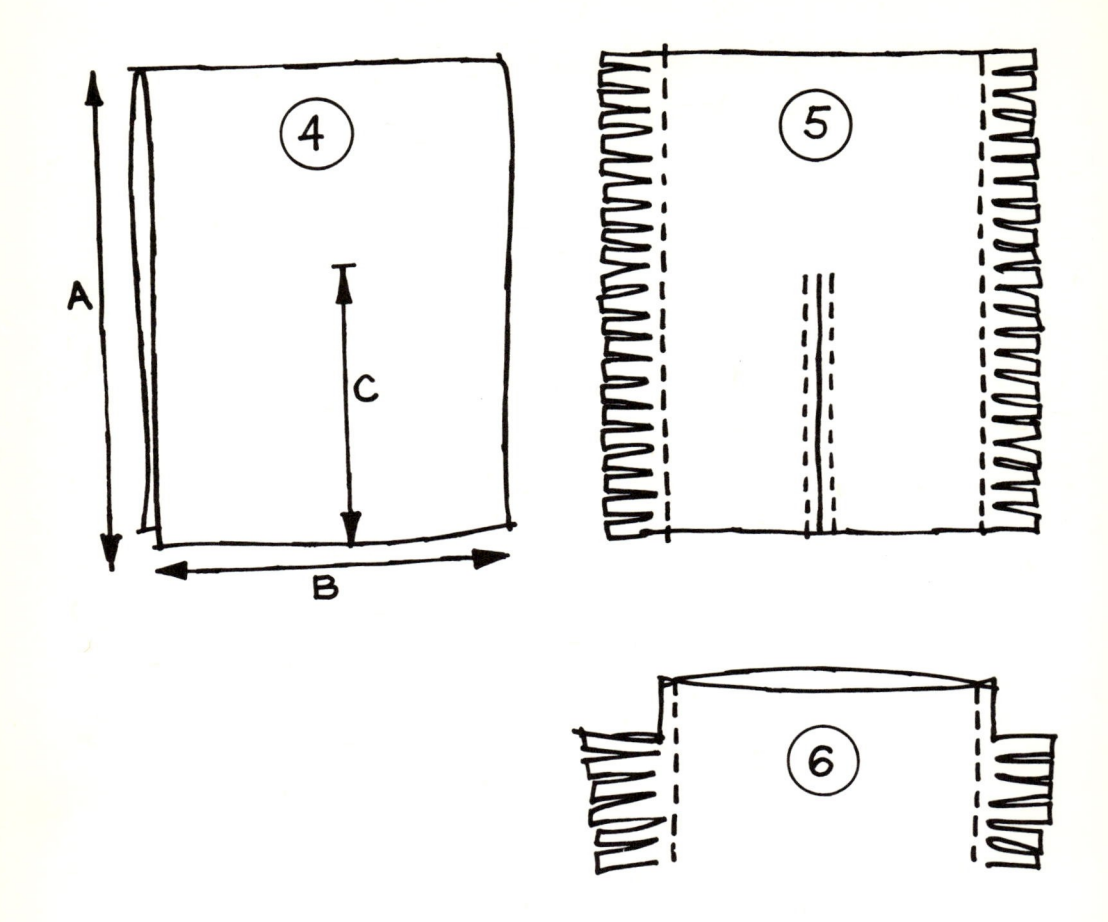

4. Cut open the top on the fold, and trim off fringe above seam (Figure 6). Turn the top edge an inch inside and sew it down. Through a side opening

88

insert the elastic, and draw it through the waistband with a safety pin (Figure 7). Pin elastic ends together.

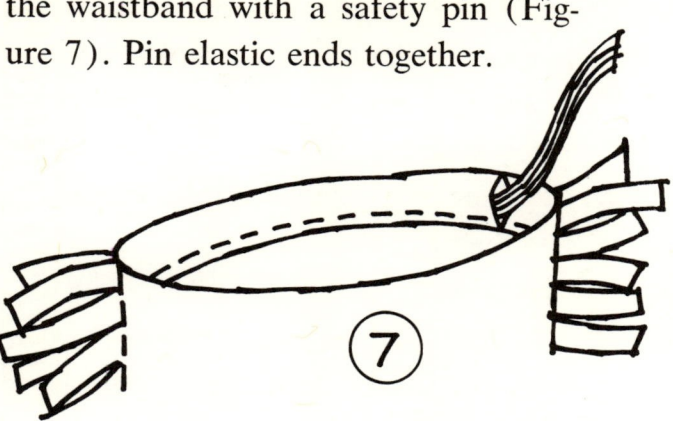

Headband:

1. Draw designs on the cardboard strip with marker or crayon (Figure 8). Fasten around your head with a paper clip or a staple.

2. Cut a feather from red paper. Cut a 1/4-inch strip of cardboard the length of the feather, and glue it on the back. From the outside edge of the feather, cut slantwise slits toward the center (Figure 9). Tape the feather to the inside of the headband.

Braids:

1. If your hair is long, part it in the middle and braid both sides. If it is short, make two braids. Cut six equal strips lengthwise from black material.

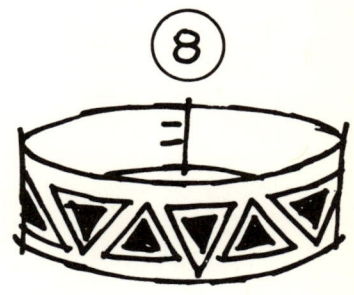

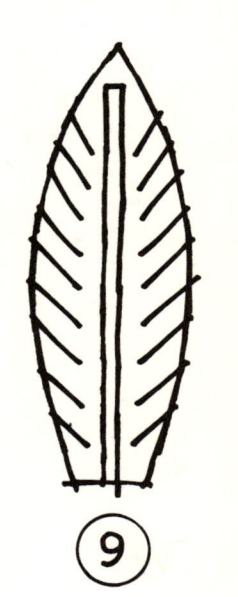

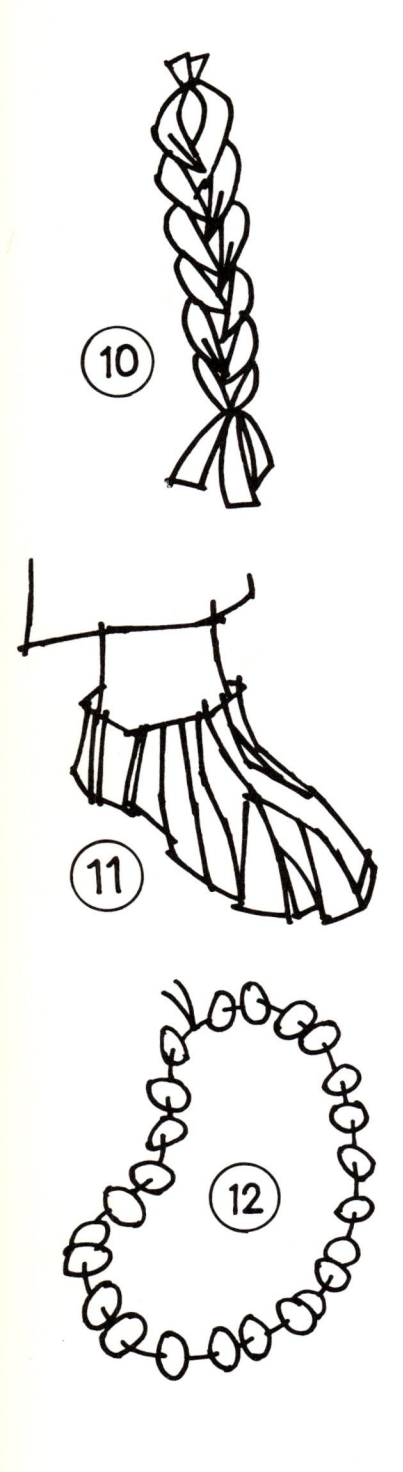

Sew three strips together at one end, and braid loosely. Sew together at the bottom (Figure 10). Make another braid the same way from the other three strips.

2. Tape the braids firmly inside the headband at the sides.

Moccasins:

1. Wear soft-leather heelless moccasins. To make moccasins, paint two pieces of foil black or brown on one side. Let the paint dry.

2. Crush a piece of foil around each foot. Cut off excess foil (Figure 11).

Beads:

1. Put a few drops of both blue and green food coloring in a bowl of water. Soak the lima beans for several hours until soft enough so a needle will go through them easily.

2. String the beans loosely on heavy sewing thread about 35 inches long. Tie the ends of the thread together (Figure 12).

DRAGON

MATERIALS:
black leotards or
   black pants and long-sleeved shirt
square piece of material,
   each side the distance
   from your shoulder to
   the tips of your fingers
strip of material,
   16 inches by 50 inches
newspapers
cellophane tape
paper bag large enough to fit
   comfortably over your head
cardboard, 3 inches by 20 inches
green paint
red paint
white paint
red construction paper
aluminum foil
household glue
black construction paper

TOOLS:
pencil
ruler
scissors
stapler
paintbrush
black crayon
white chalk

STEPS:
Body:
1. Fold the square of material in half, then in half again. At the folded

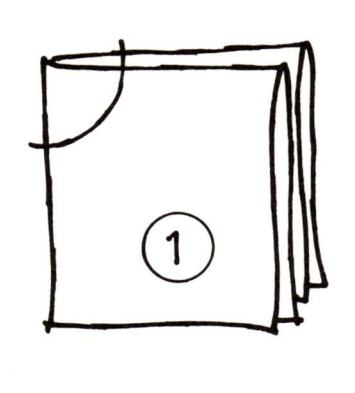

corner, measure 2½ inches down each side. Draw a curved line between marks, and cut off (Figure 1). If opening is too small to go over your head, cut off more material along the curve.

2. To make the tail, staple one end of the strip of material 8 inches up from one corner of the square. Trim the corners off the other end into a point (Figure 2).

3. Cut strips of newspaper 3 inches wide. Use colored comic strips if you don't wish to paint the dragon. These are the dragon's scales.

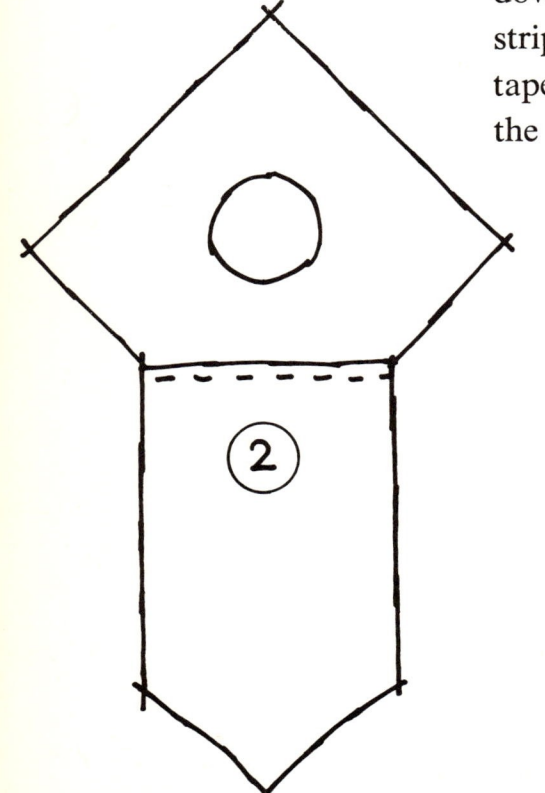

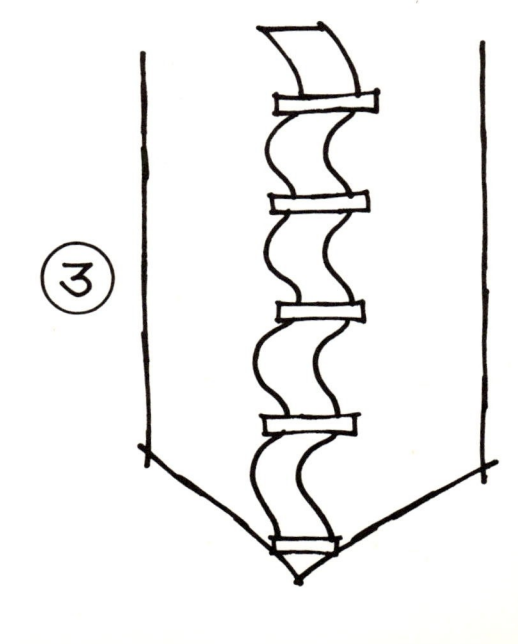

4. Beginning at the tip of the tail, tape down the end of one strip. Push the strip up a little to form a loop, and tape it down about 4 inches farther up the tail (Figure 3). Continue looping and taping down strips all the way to the opposite corner of the square. When you reach the neck opening, tape the strip down, cut off, and start again on the other side of the opening (Figure 4). Keep taping down strips close together until you have covered the entire body with scales.

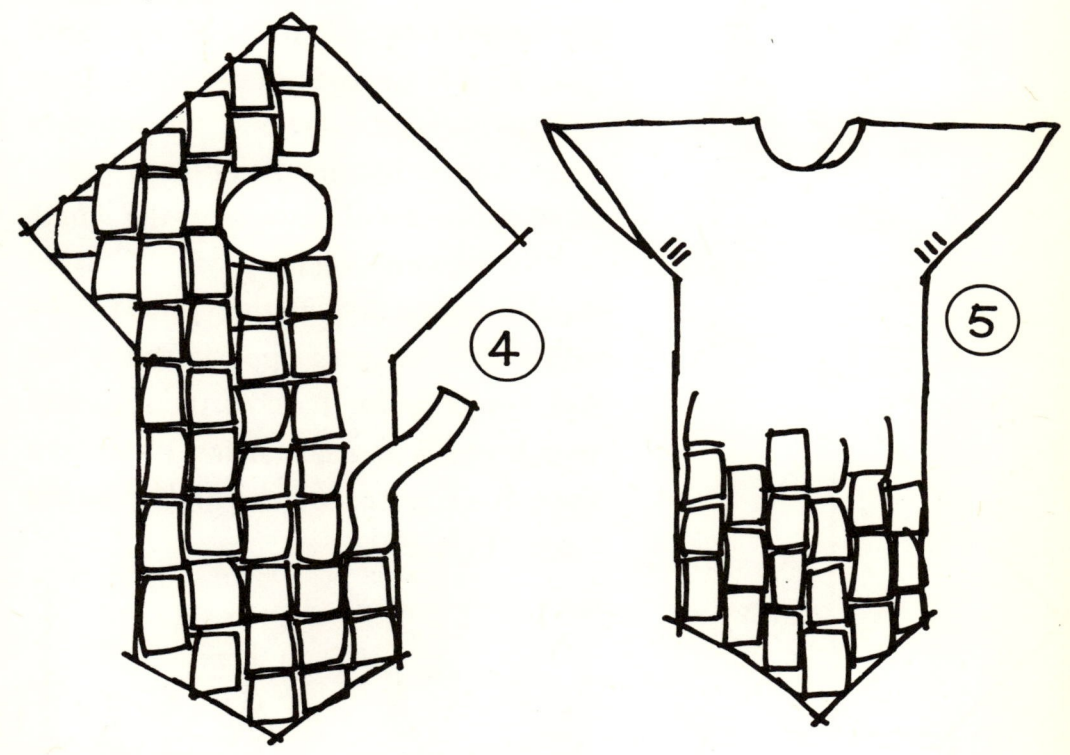

5. Fold the body square in half and staple the front and back together about halfway down the side to set the armholes (Figure 5).

93

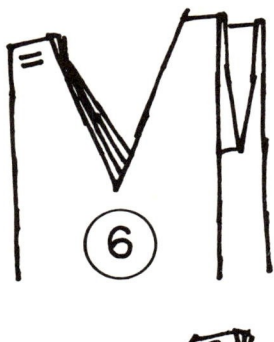

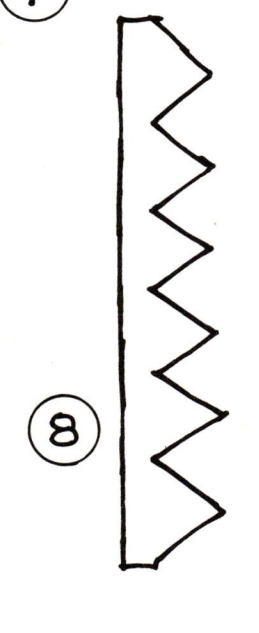

6. Paint the body green if you haven't used colored comic strips.

Head:

1. Cut a V shape at bottom of the bag, which is folded flat. Staple together at the corners; these form the dragon's ears (Figure 6).

2. Fold up the edge of bag, and put it on your head. With crayon, mark places for your eyes and mouth. Take off the bag and draw and cut out large slanted eyes and mouth (Figure 7).

3. Cut a piece of newspaper the length of the bag and 5 inches wide. Cut out spikes on one side of the paper to 1½ inches from edge of opposite side (Figure 8). Tape the base of the spikes to the dragon's head, starting above the eyes, going over the head and down the back (Figure 9).

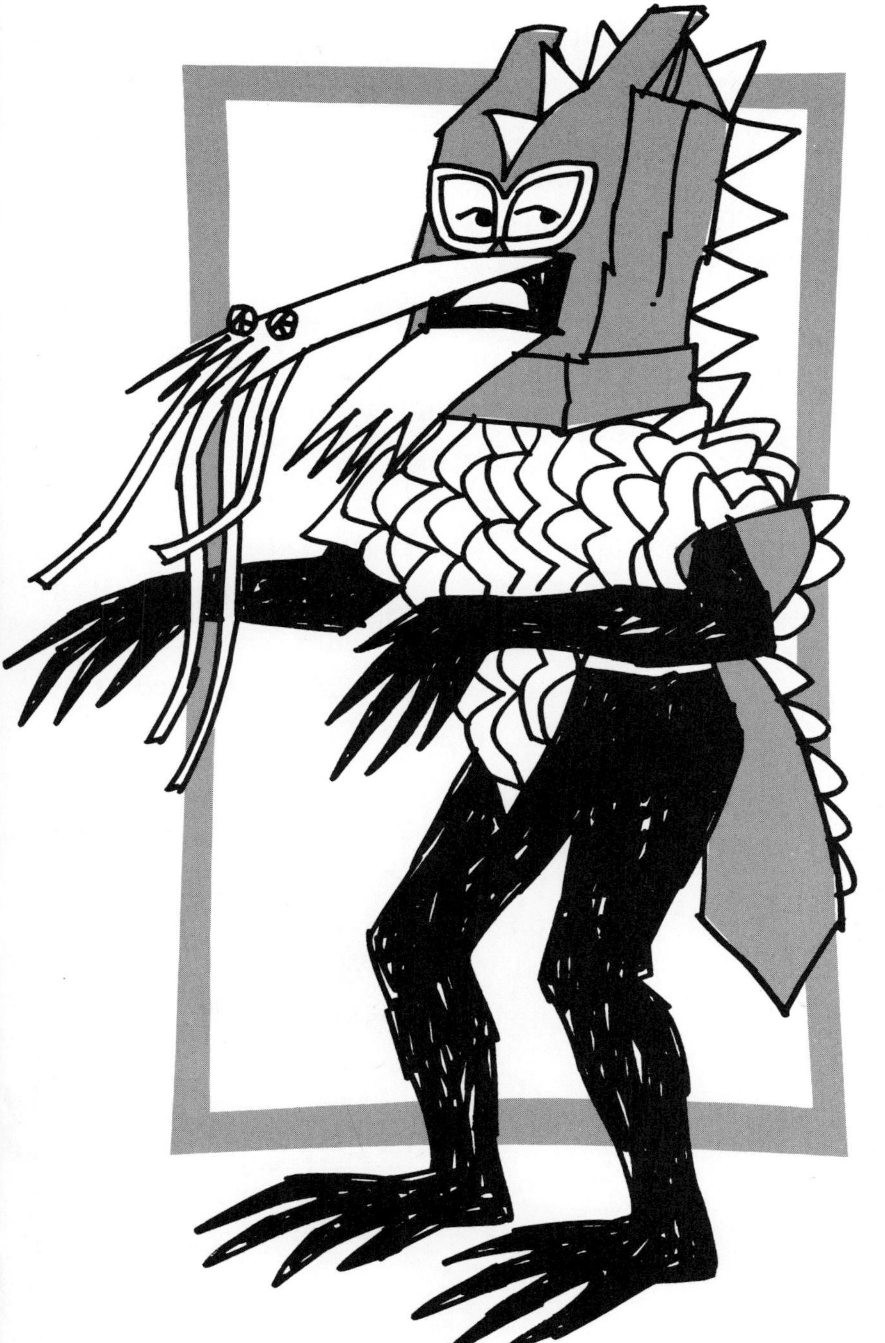

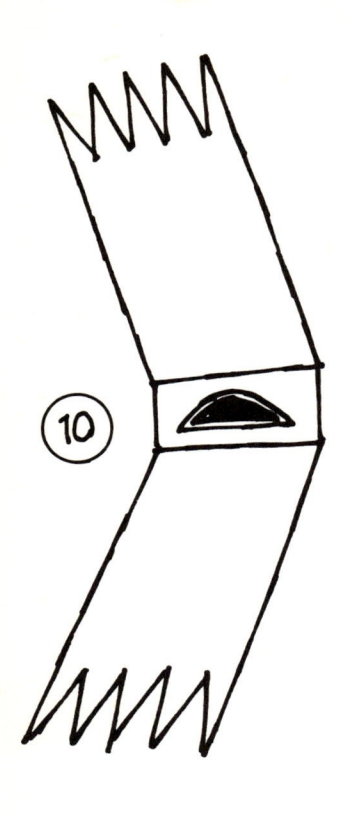

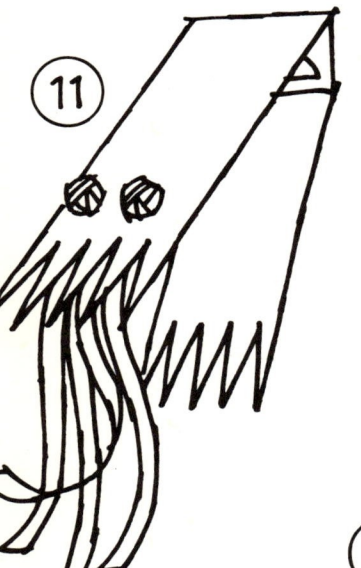

4. Cut sharp teeth along both ends of cardboard strip. Fold the cardboard in half, and cut mouth opening at fold (Figure 10). Staple or tape the strip on the bag being certain the two mouth openings line up. (The strip is the dragon's mouth and nose.)

5. Paint the head, including the outside of the mouth, green. Paint the inside of the mouth red and the teeth white. Outline the eyes with black crayon.

6. Cut several strips of red paper ¼ inch by 10 inches. Tape them inside the roof of the mouth for flames. Roll two pieces of foil into balls the size of a marble. Glue on above the teeth for nostrils (Figure 11).

Claws:

1. With white chalk, trace around your fingers on black paper, and extend each finger to a point (Figure 12). Cut out four of these claws, and tape them to your hands and feet.